PERMISSIONS

P9-CPX-721

"YoungGiftedandFat" by Sharrell D. Luckett and Rahbi Hines © 2014. Used by permission.

We thank Martin E. Segal Theatre Center for permission to republish the following essay in a modified and extended form:

Luckett, Sharrell D. "YoungGiftedandFat: Performing Transweight Identities." *The Journal of American Drama and Theatre* 26, no. 2 (2014).

ADVANCE PRAISE

Advance Praise for "YoungGiftedandFat: An Autoethnography of Size, Sexuality, & Privilege"

"In a professional analytic voice, as well as personal diary entries, Sharrell D. Luckett provides a moving and powerful voice for Black womanhood as well as white sisters preoccupied with appearance as identity. She is both funny and astute in her testimony to the power of contemporary body projects."
– Joan Jacobs Brumberg, Professor Emerita, Cornell University, NY, Author of *The Body Project: An Intimate History of American Girls* **and** *Fasting Girls: The History of Anorexia Nervosa*

"Once in every great while, a piece of work comes along that bridges the academic universe and the everyday world in ways that are intellectually important as well as palpably pragmatic. *YoungGiftedandFat* is one of those rare and important projects. With intellectually robust investigative approaches, it's hard to imagine a work that's more extensively and more genuinely inter-disciplinary than this one. The result is a superb example of the crucial connection between the personal and the political, establishing new ground in the emerging literature on the medicalization of body image as it relates to weight and the special implications that carries for women of color, in particular. Personable, accessible, boldly honest, and intellectually refreshing, this is a plain old "good read" as well as a significant addition to any of the scholarly literature dealing with "self and society," and is an impressively innovative way of re-conceptualizing the reciprocally promising relationship between artistic performance and ethnographic method."
– Kerric Harvey, Associate Professor, School of Media and Public Affairs, and Associate Director, Center for Innovative Media & the Film Studies Program, The George Washington University, Washington, DC

"*YoungGiftedandFat* tells a powerful story about the personal, relational, and cultural politics of women's body image and weight loss. Sharrell D. Luckett marshals her training as an actor, theatre and performance studies scholar, and critical autoethnographer to chart her experience of rapid weight loss, transforming from a fat Black female performing body to the performance of 'thin-ness.' This bold, honest, and beautiful book tells of both the privilege and burdens that Black women's bodies, hearts, minds, and relationships bear in contemporary culture."

– Stacy Holman Jones, Professor, Centre for Theatre and Performance, Monash University, Melbourne

"Sharrell D. Luckett is prolific as she advances the field of interdisciplinary scholarly research by writing an evocative, imperative text on the struggles and complications of being overweight in our society through her personal, poignant, and often political style. A must-have for anyone interested in performance, sexuality, African–American women's and fat studies."

– Noah Lelek, Assistant Professor and Graduate Program Coordinator in Drama, Texas Woman's University

"In *YoungGiftedandFat*, Sharrell D. Luckett provides us with a new way to enter conversations of race, body, and performance. This personal and political journey—narrated through autoethnography and personal narrative—provides a strong model of how to embed complex theoretical ideas into common narrative and dialogue. Luckett's textual creativity keeps this scholarly work interesting and opens up a space of vulnerability and critical reflection!"

– Jeffrey Q. McCune, Jr., Ph.D., Associate Professor of Women, Gender, and Sexuality Studies and African & African–American Studies, Washington University in St. Louis, MO

"With sometimes excruciating honesty, Sharrell D. Luckett provides analyses of the intersection of race, gender, and body image based in social interaction and performance theories, and provides new insight into what it means to be 'the outsider within.' Through personalizing her scholarly study and sharing her own experiences through her performance of *YoungGiftedandFat*, she gives us all cause to thoughtfully and compassionately examine our own issues and relationship with body image."

– Freda Scott Giles, Associate Professor Emerita of Theatre and African–American Studies, University of Georgia, GA, and Managing Editor, *Continuum: The Journal of African Diaspora Drama, Theatre and Performance*

YOUNGGIFTEDANDFAT

YoungGiftedandFat is a critical autoethnography of "performing thin"—on the stage and in life. Sharrell D. Luckett's story of weight loss and gain and playing the (beautiful, desirable, thin) leading lady showcases an innovative and interdisciplinary approach to issues of weight and self-esteem, performance, race, and gender. Sharrell structures her project with creative text, interviews, testimony, journal entries, dialogues, monologues, and deep theorizing through and about the abundance of flesh.

She explores the politics of Black culture, and particularly the intersections of her lived and embodied experiences. Her body and body transformation becomes a critical praxis to evidence fat as a feminist issue, fat as a Black-girl-woman issue, and fat as an ideological construct that is as much on the brain as it is on the body. *YoungGiftedandFat* is useful to any area of research or course offering taking up questions of size politics at the intersections of race and sexuality.

Sharrell D. Luckett is Assistant Professor of Theatre & Performance Studies at Muhlenberg College. Her literary and embodied research is situated in Performance Studies, African–American Studies, acting/directing theory, and Fat Studies.

Writing Lives
Ethnographic Narratives

Series Editors: Arthur P. Bochner, Carolyn Ellis, and Tony E. Adams
University of South Florida and Northeastern Illinois University

Writing Lives: Ethnographic Narratives publishes narrative representations of qualitative research projects. The series editors seek manuscripts that blur the boundaries between humanities and social sciences. We encourage novel and evocative forms of expressing concrete lived experience, including autoethnographic, literary, poetic, artistic, visual, performative, critical, multi-voiced, conversational, and co-constructed representations. We are interested in ethnographic narratives that depict local stories; employ literary modes of scene setting, dialogue, character development, and unfolding action; and include the author's critical reflections on the research and writing process, such as research ethics, alternative modes of inquiry and representation, reflexivity, and evocative storytelling. Proposals and manuscripts should be directed to abochner@usf.edu, cellis@usf.edu, or aeadams3@neiu.edu

Other volumes in this series include:

White Folks
Race and Identity in Rural America
Timothy J. Lensmire

Autobiography of a Disease
Patrick Anderson

Searching for an Autoethnographic Ethic
Stephen Andrew

For a full list of titles in this series, please visit:
https://www.routledge.com/Writing-Lives-Ethnographic-Narratives/book-series/WLEN

YOUNGGIFTEDANDFAT
An Autoethnography of Size, Sexuality, and Privilege

Sharrell D. Luckett

Routledge
Taylor & Francis Group

NEW YORK AND LONDON

First published 2018
by Routledge
711 Third Avenue, New York, NY 10017

and by Routledge
2 Park Square, Milton Park, Abingdon, Oxon, OX14 4RN

Routledge is an imprint of the Taylor & Francis Group, an informa business

© 2018 Taylor & Francis

The right of Sharrell D. Luckett to be identified as author of this work has been asserted by her in accordance with sections 77 and 78 of the Copyright, Designs and Patents Act 1988.

All rights reserved. No part of this book may be reprinted or reproduced or utilised in any form or by any electronic, mechanical, or other means, now known or hereafter invented, including photocopying and recording, or in any information storage or retrieval system, without permission in writing from the publishers.

Trademark notice: Product or corporate names may be trademarks or registered trademarks, and are used only for identification and explanation without intent to infringe.

Library of Congress Cataloging-in-Publication Data
Names: Luckett, Sharrell D., author.
Title: Younggiftedandfat : an autoethnography of size, sexuality and privilege / Sharrell D. Luckett. Other titles: Young gifted and fat
Description: New York : Routledge, 2017. | Includes bibliographical references and index.
Identifiers: LCCN 2017031432 | ISBN 9781138998827 (hardback) | ISBN 9781138038325 (pbk.) | ISBN 9781315177427 (ebook)
Subjects: LCSH: Luckett, Sharrell D. | African American actors–Biography. | College teachers–United States–Biography. | Overweight persons–United States–Biography. | Obesity–Social aspects–United States.
Classification: LCC PN2287.L755 A3 2017 | DDC 792.02/33092 [B] –dc23
LC record available at "https://protect-us.mimecast.com/s/ RKWoBRSAqqAnh6?domain=lccn.loc.gov" https://lccn.loc.gov/2017031432

ISBN: 978-1-138-99882-7 (hbk)
ISBN: 978-1-138-03832-5 (pbk)
ISBN: 978-1-315-17742-7 (ebk)

Typeset in Bembo
by Deanta Global Publishing Services, Chennai, India

THIS PROJECT IS DEDICATED TO MY MOTHER,
THE REVEREND BEVERLY H. LUCKETT,
WHO GAVE ME A "WRITING SPIRIT."
AND
GLORIA J. HARRELL,
WHOSE BASKET HAS ENOUGH ROOM FOR MY SIBLINGS AND ME.
YOUR WISDOM IS INVALUABLE.

CONTENTS

List of Images   xii
Foreword Bryant Keith Alexander   xiii
Acknowledgments   xvii
Before Pic   xx

Introduction: Contextualizing the Conundrum   1

1   Touched   30

    Talk "Fat" Session: Say It Ain't So ... Daddy Issues?   55

2   Disappearing Acts   59

3   Passing Strange   68

    Talk "Fat" Session: Fractured   89

4   Maintenance   95

5   Weighted Loss   113

    Talk "Fat" Session: Staging Life   119

6   "YoungGiftedandFat" (The Play)   127

7   Fat Girl Futurity   154

After Pic   166
Index   167

IMAGES

Front 1   Before pic – author's illustration.   *xx*
1.1   Sharrell, the early years.   54
2.1   This flyer is a creative response from Sharrell that
          speaks to her epic sense of loss after she lost weight.   67
3.1   Sharrell, the "fly" years.   87
5.1   James and Beverly Luckett, mid 1980s.   118
6.1   Sharrell as herself in "YoungGiftedandFat."   152
Back 1   After pic – author's illustration.   166

FOREWORD

Bryant Keith Alexander

The phrase, "to be young, gifted, and Black" has almost become a mainstay in the Black vernacular, *signaling* the abundance of talent and intellect in Black communities around the world; *signifying* on talent and intellect that rightfully finds a forum on stages of public recognition, and between the pages of journals and books as evidence of the Black literati and intelligentsia. And in many ways the phrase becomes a *signification* of everyday Black cultural life; in the riffing rhythms of Black talk in kitchens or barbershop and salons, in the linguistic turns and rapier wit of playing the dozens, in the rhymes of Black girls playing Double Dutch in which feet are connected to tongues to rhythms and rhymes that are not just playful but performative—playful calisthenics as a performance of culture and strategies for living. In the midst of it all, borrowing a theme from Countee Cullen's famous poem, "Yet Do I Marvel," as he compares his struggles as a Black poet to that of characters in Greek mythology (namely Tantalus and Sisyphus)—the realization of being "young, gifted, and Black" is in the struggle of being as site and state of resistance, resilience, and the righteousness in Black joy. Which is to marvel. And while the powerful messaging of the phrase, "to be young, gifted, and Black" defies age it is most salient in the kids singing in the church or school choir learning and teaching lessons about how to practice voice; in the young Black activist practicing her resistance in learning to say no—critically—and learning to say yes—optimistically—and learning the difference between dancing and marching to and against the politics of the times. It's in the ebb and flow, and beauty of Black cultural life, and as Maya Angelou would say, "It's in the reach of my arms, the span of my hips, the stride of my step, the curl of my lips." And, of course, she was poetically theorizing about the body politic of the Black "*Phenomenal Woman.*"

The phrase "to be young, gifted, and Black" is both public acknowledgment and private words whispered in the ears of sleeping Black babies. It lives in the assumed banality of the everyday and the greatest of public achievements, but is made palpable when Black artists and scholars use their lived experience as the source material of their scholarship and their artistry; theorizing on the complexity of Black cultural life not to prove a point, but to point to proof of our beautiful and heroic existence. The phrase also turns as both a description and a critique, a commentary on unfilled potentials and *dreams deferred*, as a brother Langston Hughes might state. Finding itself located in the lexicon of celebrating and mourning, of remembrance and resistance, of looking back in order to look forward.

The phrase "to be young, gifted, and Black" signals that song, you know, the one sung by Nina Simone in memory of Lorraine Hansberry, that Black girl who took Broadway by storm by telling a story of *A Raisin in the Sun*—a story of the trials, tribulations, and triumphs of a Black family; a story that was particular and universal, a story of the human spirit told through the frame of a Black family—whether white people wanted to see their humanity through a Black lens or not. You know that song that Nina Simone sings with lyrics that say: "In the whole world you know there are billion boys and girls, who are young, gifted, and Black, and that's a fact! Young, gifted, and Black. We must begin to tell our young there's a world waiting for you. This is a quest that's just begun" (Simone 1969). I know that song as a mantra and memorial; that song as testament and treatise; and that phrase that almost does not fully realize its completion as if to say, "To be young, gifted, and Black is …"—signaling the openness of possibility.

Sharrell D. Luckett structures her book, *YoungGiftedandFat*, with creative text, interviews, testimony, journal entries, dialogues, poetry, monologues, and deep theorizing through and about her abundance; which is partially about her flesh but maybe more so about her spirit. Luckett riffs on the politics of Black culture, and particularly on the intersections of her lived and embodied experiences as a Blackgirlwoman, in a Blackgirlwoman's body; the negotiations and embodiedness of being through her own theories of the flesh. Like her name claiming two *rs*, two *ls*, and two *ts*, *Sharrell D. Luckett* takes up space on the page and on the stages of everyday life, but with a poeticism of movement and grace—like most of the Black women in her life, and even in my own life.

When Cherríe Moraga talked about *theories of/in the flesh*, she is talking about a critical positionality enlivened by the necessity to give voice to the particularity of lived experience. She is talking, writing, theorizing about that location "where the physical realities of our lives—our skin color, the land or concrete we grew up on, our sexual longings—all fuse to create a politic born out of necessity" (Moraga and Anzaldúa 1981, 23). And when D. Soyini Madison (1993) references *theories of the flesh* through Black feminist thought, she is talking about strategies of social engagement that establish spaces of possibility and transformation. For her, "theories of the flesh reflect the distinctive interpretations of the world carved out of the material realities of a group's life experiences. Specialized knowledge infuses elements and themes of Black women's culture and traditions with critical interventionist thinking to provide Black women with new tools of resistance" (213).

Sharrell D. Luckett is talking about the same things in theory and practice—and she takes it literally to the flesh; she takes it to fat as an excess of flesh—her body (and body transformation) becomes a critical praxis to evidence fat as a feminist issue, fat as a Black-girl-woman issue, fat as an ideological construct that is as much on the brain as it is on the body. She is theorizing fat as physical, psychological, and political struggle—taking up headspace as much as physical space. In the process, she looks at the Black female body in its historically social construction—as "*skin deep*, as it emphasizes the most superficial versions of Black women, and *skin tight*, as it has proved to be nearly inescapable, even in Black women's self-conception and self-representation" (Wallace-Sanders 2002, 4). In many ways, Dr. Luckett gives subtle tribute and rescue to our sister Saartjie Baartman, whose abundance as a Black/African/female/body was made in/famous as a reluctant Black Venus under the White gaze of slavery.

Amongst many fields of knowing and theorizing, Dr. Luckett's work draws from *Theatre Studies, Performance Studies, Communication Studies, Cultural Studies, Black Studies, Black Feminism, Sociology,* and *Fat Studies.* That is some fancy-ass way of saying that she is theorizing about the politics of her own identity through multiple discourses and prisms of seeing and being seen. In my own words, respectfully applied, Dr. Luckett is talking about being a fat chick, then a thin chick, and the politics of desire, sex, and sexuality that go along with that struggle on the stages of everyday life. She is writing about the struggle of how bodies relate to other bodies in place (vertically or horizontally); about how bodies relate to other bodies in space (those practiced places of home, family, and relationships); about how bodies hump and haunt other bodies (in the light of day and in the darkness of dreams and desire); about the dis-ease and disease of bodies that force us all to regulate weight in relation to the social perception of bodies (desirable spectacle or freak show), in relation to our sense of self, in relation to life and death; about how bodies are read as accessible and acceptable in the reading of difference—and what people want to see and believe in—both in the *make-believe world of theatre* or the *making-belief reality of performance*. She is talking about the ephemeral nature of bodies, the mutability of bodies, the disposability of bodies, and the forebodedness of bodies—as in the fearful apprehension of being and becoming. In each case, bodies long to be rescued by the freed mind of one's own consciousness that grants the permission to love the self, first.

The *YoungGiftedandFat* project blends the borders of meaning and embodies the prophesy of possibility. In many ways, the title of the book is a tribute to Nina and Lorraine, and a testament to every Blackgirlwoman who ever questioned the relationship between her gifts, her intellect, and her fat—as if one dis-informs the other. Through her own intellectual and academic privilege, Sharrell D. Luckett funnels the phantasms of fat in/as performance; in/as scholarship to poetically theorize on her own lived experiences—turning her presumed deficit into asset. In the process, she bleeds the borders between the pages and the stages of public theatres as laboratories of culture, and academic writing as the critical articulation of voice, to evidence the promise of the Black intelligentsia to theorize on everyday Black cultural issues, giving it roots and wings. This book demands not just a reading perspective but an audiencing perspective—as does any good autoethnography that unfolds through performative writing, forcing the reader to both witness the critical crafting of lived experience and to witness the unfolding of those stories in the telling of the told that performance helps to materialize. The accessibility of this project to diverse readers speaks not only to Sharrell D. Luckett's writing, but also to the universality of the story/struggle—the autoethnography of her experience as someone who is young, gifted, and *fat*; but also as someone who helps to further establish a template, through method and mode; of how we (the readers) might all further explore the tortures of our own travels in living, and how we can become triumphant in telling lived experience.

– Bryant Keith Alexander, Ph.D., Professor and Dean, College of Communication and Fine Arts, Loyola Marymount University, CA

ACKNOWLEDGMENTS

God: the energy that made me, and the one who grades me. I do appreciate all of the make-up exams and extra credit opportunities, but please no more pop-quizzes. Thank ya big God!

Thank you to my family for their immeasurable support: Jamia, Jay, Derrick, Carles, Uncle Clarence Luckett and family, Pompano Beach family (Aunt Connie, Aunt Deedee, Aunt Jackie, Aunt Gloria, Uncle Nathaniel, Uncle Richard), Tomah Joe, Evelyn Davis, Bobo, Gadget, and Ellery Queen; the Hines and the Shaffers.

Carolyn Ellis, thank you so much for blessing this project. Your close, critical feedback and support is bountifully appreciated. The *Writing Lives: Ethnographic Narratives* series is a gift to the world. I am truly humbled to be in the company of this exceptional group of scholars.

Bryant Keith Alexander, my mentor and colleague, the profundity of your scholarship and your presence in my academic journey is greatly appreciated. Thank you for your critical insights, readings, and conversations. You are a true gem.

M. Heather Carver, thank you for modeling what it means to be an outstanding professor, mentor, colleague, scholar, and performing artist all at the same time. Thank you for believing in me, being an awesome listener, and laughing with me through the craziness. You are a woman of indomitable spirit, and I am grateful to have studied with you.

Mary Weems, your feedback, edits, and wealth of knowledge proved invaluable. Thank you for your time and talents.

To: Rahbi Hines who is my other half, R. Carmichael who is always present, Tia Shaffer who shares her talents, J. Michael Kinsey who talks me off the ledge, Ashleigh Dillard who taught me how to fight, Jeffrey Dickerson who is always so gracious with his genius, Juel D. Lane who can hold water and embody it at the same time, Guy Thorne who dances with me though I can't keep up, Richard Majek who teaches me Yoruba, Tomah Joe who held my mama's hand, Jonathan Lassiter whose friendship and listening ear I value, Sharisa Whatley who is a gifted playwright, Charity Jordan who gave me a healing CD, Justin Jordan who called after I left, Jeb Middlebrook for his activism and survival parties, Jane Lee who makes me feel sane, Noah Lelek who calms me down, Benjamin Mathes who is amazing, Marisa Commisso who escaped with me, Jabari Ali who believes in me, Alisa Porter who is the best boss ever, R. Rogers who won the snowball fight, John Reed who is supportive, Khalia Parker who is a gem, Rikki Byrd whose artistry moves mountains, 4-year-old Eden who would call to check on me at 5 a.m., Choyce who is ebullient, Patrease Rae who shares her beauty, Esther Terry who keeps in touch, A. Nicole who encouraged me, Victoria S. and Anaya who studied and laughed with me, Victoria Washington who always graces me with her presence, Torwa Joe who is my first best friend, Maiesha McQueen who is ever loving, Ife Okwumabua who helped me water my garden, Enisha Brewster who takes amazing leaps and pictures, Cecille Bolton, Reggie Jones, and Dara Harris for being consistent, loving friends; you are all wonderful, extraordinary beings, and I am so blessed to have shared space with you. I wish you all much success.

SWMM, I'm so appreciative of the cheering and celebrations, always: Denise Hart, Kashi Johnson, Shondrika Moss-Bouldin, and Daphnie Sicre. Ya'll are rockstars.

My work has been uplifted and honored in various ways by some amazing people who gave of their time to endorse this project. Thank you to Bryant Keith Alexander, Stephanie Batiste, Joan Jacobs Brumberg, M. Heather Carver, Kathryn Ervin, Freda Scott Giles, Stacy Holman Jones, Kerric Harvey, Mark Hein, Sander Gilman, Noah Lelek, Jeffrey McCune, Tamara Rawitt, Kenan Thompson, and Sara Warner.

Many thanks to my academic mentors and colleagues who have supported this research: Shirlene Holmes, Carol T. Scott, Freddie Hendricks, Clyde Ruffin, Matt Saltzberg, Rickerby Hinds, Kerric Harvey, Jeb Middlebrook, Jane Lee, Sandra Adell, Debi Barber, Corina Benavides López, Cheryl Black,

Art Bochner, Kevin Brown, Suzanne Burgoyne, Misty DeBerry, Kathryn Ervin, Munashe Furusa, Freda Scott Giles, Anne Harris, Kelly Herman, E. Patrick Johnson, A. Kpodar, Gary Kuwahara, and Ramón Rivera-Servera.

There were several institutions that supported my research throughout the writing and performing of this project. Thank you to the University of Missouri-Columbia, Harvard University's Mellon School of Theater and Performance Research, Northwestern University's Mellon Institute of Black Feminist Performance, Cornell University, Muhlenberg College, The New School, Parsons School of Design, St. Lawrence University, California State University-Dominguez Hills, Georgia State University, Columbus State University, the Greater Solid Rock Baptist Church, and the Youth Ensemble of Atlanta.

To my colleagues at Muhlenberg College, it is a pleasure to work with so many wonderful artists every day. Thank you for your support on my academic journey.

To Hannah Shakespeare, Matt Bickerton, and the staff at Routledge Publishing, it has been great working with you.

And finally, thank you to my amazing students (too many to name). I am so honored and grateful to have taught you. And I have learned so much from you all as well. Many of you have flourished into stellar performers, academics, parents, and mentors. I am proud. Keep pushing.

Megan J. Stewart and Audrey Edwards (Augan and Medrey), I couldn't have done this without you. Thank you for listening, rehearsing, and having my back. Your futures are so bright (right now). And Sean Cook, I see your greatness; keep shining. Love you all.

BEFORE PIC

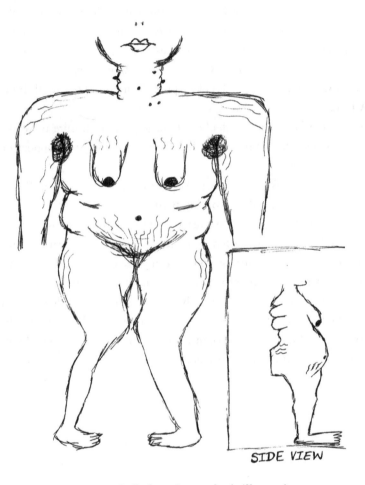

SIDE VIEW

Figure Front 1: Before pic – author's illustration.

July 26, 2000, Age 20

Dear Diary,

I hate myself because I am fat. I'm not even pretty anymore. All I wanted out of life was to be slim and cross my legs. I'll never have a man who is in love with me. Men just don't like fat women. I feel like shit. I try to act like I love myself, but I really don't. I would give anything to be small. I got my hair done today, but I didn't see pretty. I am dreading going to school or church because it feels like I lost and everyone is watching me because of my weight. I like food, but it's killing me. I am starting to hate myself again. Men don't like me and I don't like me. But I'm all that I have. So I have to put on fake smiles and I don't like to go places in public. Obesity is not a disease that everyone sees. I long to wear tank tops and tight jeans and women's apparel. All I wear are dark t-shirts and stretch pants. My legs are huge. My thighs, and my arms, and my once cute face too. I'm tired of being depressed. I wish to God that I was slim.

INTRODUCTION

CONTEXTUALIZING THE CONUNDRUM

> The body will tell the truth when all else fails, with or without you.
>
> *Misty DeBerry, Performance Artist*[1]

Nine years ago I lived as a fat Black female actress and teacher, trying to learn to love my curves and maintain a healthy lifestyle.[2] I was failing miserably. I ate McDonald's and Zaxby's nearly every day, coupled with home-cooked meals. I imagined myself unattractive, undesirable, and unworthy of love and attention from men. At the same time, through weight loss advertisements, public ridicule, and size discrimination, society made it very clear that I was the gross unwanted "other."

In America, a fat person is often classified as diseased, one who must be cured of a pathological and physical illness. Cultural historian Sander Gilman has noted, "Obesity presents itself today in the form of a 'moral panic'—that is, an 'episode, condition, person or group of persons' that have in recent times been 'defined as a threat to societal values and interests.'"[3] In addition, physicians argue that a fat body creates exorbitant health costs and is directly correlated with mortality risks.[4] For instance, as I began to approach 300 lbs. my body was classified as morbidly obese, and my largeness became unbearable and was cited as the root of my physical ailments.

To add to my conundrum, my being female exacerbated the abject ostracism. In *Fat Is a Feminist Issue* Susie Orbach speaks to the fact that women incur more issues with fat than men do, while sociologists and cultural observers assert that the size and appearance of one's body determines marriageability, upward mobility, and/or perceived attractiveness, especially for women.[5] Subtending these claims, I experienced size prejudice early in my dating efforts when boys began to tell me they weren't romantically interested in me because I was fat: "I don't like big girls." "I look at chubby girls like they my sister." "You're too big." "How much you weigh?" Thus, I sought out opportunities to talk to boys on the phone that had never seen me before. I accomplished this by signing up for telephone dating services or obtaining boys' telephone numbers from my best friend's phone book.

> "Hey, so when we gone meet up?" the boys usually asked.
> "I'm really busy with school."
> "What you look like? You fat? I don't fuck with fat girls."
> Scared. "I'm cute." Hoping we would change subjects.
> "Your voice don't sound like a fat girl's voice. You sound sexy.
> There ain't no way you can be fat."

To make matters even worse, I'm an 80s baby, meaning I grew up in an era where there was little access to girly looking clothes and colors for fat female children and teens, denying me the label of feminine. I had to shop in the big and tall men's section, and my mom eventually hired a seamstress to make dresses for me so I could "properly" perform what is often coded as feminine. In her essay, "Foucault, Femininity, and the Modernization of Patriarchal Power," Sandra Lee Bartky wrote, "To have a body felt to be 'feminine'—a body socially constructed through the appropriate practices—is in most cases crucial to a woman's sense of herself as female."[6] The fact that the fashion industry did not make clothes for my size as a child and pre-teen provided me with a clear sign that my body was abnormal, and even though plus-size clothing became available in my early adult years, the message was ingrained: fat females are unacceptable citizens who are not authentically feminine. To add, Bartky correlated slenderness with femininity, as she argued that "The disciplinary project of femininity is a 'setup': it requires such radical and extensive measures of bodily transformation that virtually every woman who gives herself to it is destined in some degree to fail."[7] Still, Gilman noted, "diet we must ... to be saved."[8]

Yet, losing weight is extremely difficult, and even if this nigh-impossible feat is accomplished, only 5% of people who achieve substantial weight loss are able to keep the weight off for long periods of time, thereby making extreme weight loss a remarkable feat.[9]

As my dieting failures multiplied, the constant, disapproving scrutiny of the world affected my well-being, and I spiraled into a deep depression. My doomed quest to achieve "normal" weight was never-ending. My depressive state of failure rendered me hopeless. The sadder I got, the bigger I grew, until I experienced my first nosebleed. The illness of my body must have scared me skinny because only a few months later I enrolled in a medically supervised 800-calorie-per-day diet program and lost nearly 100 pounds within eight months. Having succumbed to the physical and mental attacks from society by nearly starving myself, I crossed one of the most contentious, palpable borders known to most women in America: the border that separates fat from skinny. My new body serves as a document of acceptance, my "passport," if you will, into a new privileged "home" of thin women.

In this project I position myself as a weight loss sufferer and survivor, telling stories from my childhood and adult years via autoethnography, a research method and methodology in which the self is critically explored and excavated to better understand and connect with others within a cultural context.[10] I reveal how my journey from a morbidly obese woman to a slender[11] woman shaped my awareness of my *outsider-within* identity as a Black woman, a performance artist, and scholar. Coined by Patricia Hill Collins, an outsider-within identity initially referenced the social location of Black women in the field of domesticated work.[12] In this book I use the construct of outsider-within identity as a theoretical frame to explore what it means to be a fat Black woman living within a privileged body or "home." I also explore how straddling vastly different physical and psychological identities led me to engage what I term *transweight* performance. Transweight performance for me references both a mode of reflection and the subject of reflection linked to the relationship between weight loss and identity construction. It serves as a means of understanding this experience for myself and as a means of communicating and perhaps illuminating such experience for others.

Just as the Latin prefix "trans" has been attached to various identity markers to signify crossing from one condition or location to another, as in *transnational* or *transgender*, I employ *transweight* as a term to identify someone who acquires a new size identity by losing or gaining a large amount of weight in a short amount of time, signaling unchartered possibilities of temporal and spatial fluidities in studies dealing with the flesh, the female, and the fat.[13] Further, as an American woman of African descent, I theoretically map my use of the prefix "trans" through and within the transatlantic slave trade, as many of my ancestors were transported against their will while subsequently transitioning from human to subhuman and/or gendered to ungendered.[14] In this way, my use of the prefix "trans" intimates the acknowledgment that descendants of the enslaved have always been marked in such a way. Thus the "trans" phenomenon being associated with transitioning and evolving bodies is not new. Though I value the conversation and contributions to "trans" theory from LGBTQA+ constituencies, I approach my journey and this autoethnography through a critical race lens of critique. With my use of the prefix "trans" I aim to further open up the conversation surrounding the types of bodies that were enslaved, including those who possessed weighted identities within their communities.

As I offer insight into the psychological and physiological health of a Black female who has been both morbidly obese and slender, the questions I explore are: What occurs when the fat Black female performing body transforms to slender and then engages in the performance of "thin-ness?" What are the implications of a Black female body that physically "passes" in a new way? What happens when a formerly fat, Black body experiences "double consciousness" in a historically new way: a way in which how the "other" sees the body affords that body a privilege that is unfamiliar, abounding with social and cultural perks. Unraveling my experience with extreme weight loss, I offer my slender palimpsest of a body as an entryway into a culture and world largely unexplored.

DISCOVERING THE DEPTH

In her 1999 dissertation, "The Poetics of Excess: Images of Large Women on Stage and Screen," Claire Van Ens lists five stereotypical film roles played by large actresses: The Butch, Bitch Lesbian; The Dowdy Dowager; One of the Boys; The Asexual/Non-Woman; and The Maternal Earth-Mother.[15] Not surprisingly, throughout high school and well into my undergrad studies at the University of Georgia and Georgia State University, I was usually cast in the aforementioned roles as a fat stage actress.

Having trained as an actress with Freddie Hendricks in the Hendricks Method, regardless of stereotypes often ascribed to fat bodies, I was taught to bring truth and focus to each role.[16] In accord with Constantin Stanislavski, Uta Hagen, Sanford Meisner, and other acting theorists, Hendricks suggested that to play a character truthfully onstage, one has to know and believe in her "real" self.[17] Of course, my sense of self and "truth" was uniquely altered after I lost weight. Complicating the weight loss experience was my move from Atlanta, Georgia to Columbia, Missouri to pursue a doctorate degree in Theatre and Performance Studies at the University of Missouri, Columbia. This relocation was key to me discovering the extent of my conundrum because I was living and studying around people who did not know me or my fat past. However, it wasn't until I auditioned for a university play that I became aware of the serious effects and implications of my extreme weight loss.

During the fall of my first year as a doctoral student, I auditioned for *Holding Up the Sky*, a world premiere adaptation of Earth creation stories written by the Grammy nominated storyteller, Milbre Burch. I was cast as the Young Woman, the leading female role; a role that required a beautiful, slender young actress. This casting is when I recognized that though I was rightfully perceived as a slender Black female by my professors and peers, I still processed my encounters both on and off the stage as a morbidly obese Black female. I did not believe myself to be a slender woman, so I felt as though I was performing slenderness and femininity in life or in the virtual reality of the stage. Preparing for the role proved frustrating, as I had lost my sense of identity. Identity is critical to an actor as Uta Hagen explains; "First you must learn to know who *you* are. You must find your own sense of identity, enlarge this sense of self, and learn to see how that knowledge can be put to use in the characters you will portray on stage."[18] As one can imagine, my changed body caused identity ambiguity because I was viewed and treated as an entirely different person. I transformed from physically inferior to physically elite, from ugly to attractive, and from undesirable to desirable. My body now read as happy, healthy, and worthy of protection. As an actress I went from mammy to mother (or wife), and from asexual, ensemble roles to sexy leading roles. My work in *Holding Up the Sky* led me to suffer from heightened psychological and physical stress because of my history as a morbidly obese person and my lack of experience on stage in a newly transformed, feminine body. For instance, I started to experience extreme anxiety when I was told that my costume would reveal a large amount of skin, that I had to dance and be lifted in the show, and that I had to simulate sex onstage with an orgasm.

★★★

Her gray office door was open so I peeped my head in. "Dr. Carver?" I murmured as so not to disturb her typing on her computer.

"Aaaaahaahaa!" The theatre professor and woman who would
eventually become my dissertation Chair let out a laugh that I
had to respond to.

I laughed a little too. "Hahahaha." Not knowing why we were
laughing.

"Call me Heather. Heather is fine." She pressed her closed lips
together making a mini friendly smile.

"Ok, Heather or Dr. Heather?" I suggested as I stood in the
threshold of her door. I just wasn't comfortable not using formal titles. Maybe it was the southern manners I had brought
with me to the midwest.

The bookshelves in her office almost touched the ceiling and were packed
with various texts, papers, and apparent dissertations.

"Come in, come on in," she said while standing up and shifting books
around to reach a metal rolling chair with books and newspapers placed in its
seat. I finally acknowledged she was damn near 6 ft. Slightly interesting that
both of the most influential professors in my higher education studies are very
tall women, and both have won courageous battles with cancer. Dr. Shirlene
Holmes, a theatre professor and prolific playwright whom I studied with at
Georgia State University is a 5'10" tall Black woman who has beat five bouts
of cancer, and now I would form a close relationship with Dr. Heather Carver
who battled stage 4 breast cancer, and developed a trilogy of intriguing solo
shows that discuss her experience; *Booby Prize: A Comedy about Breast Cancer*,
Booby Trap: A Hair-Raising Experience, and *Booby Hatch: A Hysterical Musical(e)*.

After she rolled the chair closer to me and welcomed me further into her
office, she looked back up at me. "Have a seat. Wussup?" Her honey blonde
shoulder-length hair seemed damp as if she just washed it after a workout.
The sun shone through the lone window on her pale face with natural
blushed cheeks.

I stayed standing with her. "Dr. Heather I was cast in *Holding Up
the Sky*.

"Yes, yes, I know. Congrats. That's awesome."

I flashed an unsure smile. "Thank you." The weight of my forest
green JanSport bookbag began to irritate my shoulders so I
took it off and laid it in the chair seat, while Dr. Heather sat
back down at her desk.

Smiling and sensing something was the matter, my professor
became a bit more serious. "Wussup?"
"I was just stopping by because ... ." Noticing her eyes blinking.
"Because ... cause I was ... ummm ... I was fat before I came
here and this is all weird to me."
She managed to keep a straight face. Then blurted out, "Ok."
I was relieved a little. "Ok?"

She let out a laugh that sounded like it hurt her throat. A laugh that one can't
ignore. A laugh that beckons a laugh in return.

"Hahahaha." Not knowing why we were laughing. "Yeah, I just
don't want to tell the director."
"Then don't."
"You think it's ok?"
"Sharrell you will be fine."
Still unsure, but reaching to pick up my book bag. "Ok, it's just
that ... it's just that ..."
She cut me off. "You know what you should do?" Her face got
real serious.
"What?"
"You should keep a journal."
"I already do that." I blurted out. I was still in high school
teacher mode and perhaps a bit too confident about my
artistic repertoire I brought with me after 6 years of formally
teaching high school theatre, and running a non-profit theatre
program for teens in my spare time. I probably shouldn't have
signaled that her advice to write wasn't helpful. I didn't mean
it that way, I thought. But she responded cooly.
"Well great, that's even better." Pause. "Do you write about your
weight stuff?"
"A little bit."
"Well write more." She let out another big laugh.
"Ok." Half smiling while trying to put my finger on her personality. "Ok. Ok. I will just journal more."
In a high-pitched voice that reminded me of Marge Simpson
from The Simpsons. "Good. How is everything else going?
You settled in?"

"Yes, yes." Releasing a deep breath. "Well that's all I wanted. Thanks
  Dr. Heather."

"Sure thing. See you around."

★★★

After "coming out" to Dr. Heather, I decided to keep my "real" identity a
secret to others in order to "pass" daily as a slender, feminine person. I now
was fully aware of my performance of slenderness that others perceived to
be true. Communications and Performance Studies scholar Bryant Keith
Alexander reminds us that passing is a collaborative process. Passing doesn't
happen unless somebody thinks it's real.[19] And as I became invested in the
process of "passing" I quickly learned that the easiest way to effectively
"pass" as a slender female was to enact rehearsed femininity. Judith Butler
has argued that femininity is a "mode of enacting and reenacting received
gender norms which surface as so many styles of flesh."[20] So though I did
not believe myself to be feminine, I certainly knew how to perform the gestural repertoire of femininity thanks to the media and other bodies labeled
as feminine. During this time, I also became aware that I was accessing thin
privilege, which occurs when one receives special benefits and treatment
because of one's thinness. Passing as slender and feminine began to provide
a sense of normalcy for me as a doctoral student and actress. Following Dr.
Heather's suggestion, I began journaling more frequently, with an express
focus on capturing my peculiar experiences and encounters.

My autoethnographic research was extended further when I was cast as
Rose Maxson in August Wilson's *Fences* just a year later. Participating in both
university plays proved excellent opportunities to study my processes and
performances interwoven in a complex journey of learning to inhabit a new
body and believably performing slenderness and femininity on and off the
stage. As I experienced fat and thin, unprivileged and privileged, separately, I
purposefully created art and wrote towards a desegregation of identity.

No Curves Allowed: Black Women Too

In the past decade there has been a proliferation of studies on the Black female
performing body, including Uri McMillan's *Embodied Avatars: Genealogies of
Black Feminist Art and Performance* (2015), which excavates Black women's
contributions and lineage in performance art; Mireille Miller-Young's *A
Taste for Brown Sugar: Black Women in Pornography* (2014), an expansively rich

study and archive of Black women's participation in adult entertainment; *solo/black/woman: scripts, interviews, and essays* (2014), an anthology that deftly curates Black feminist solo performance, edited by E. Patrick Johnson and Ramón Rivera-Servera; *Troubling Vision: Performance, Visuality, and Blackness* (2011) by Nicole Fleetwood, which considers the visual commodity of Black bodies; and *Embodying Black Experience: Stillness, Critical Memory, and the Black Body* (2010) by Harvey Young, which investigates the Black performative body in various socio–political contexts.[21] While these works are all significant studies that explore the Black female performing body, none focus specifically on the issue of weight, or the performance of "weighted" (fat/thin) identities.

This lack of literature on the Black/female/transweight performative body is most likely due to the absence of Black transweight women writing about and/or performing weight loss, and can also be attributed to the fact that the fat body rarely transforms. Thus, my autoethnography aims to carve out a space in the public and academic sphere for the transweight Black female, one that is intensely personal and profoundly political.

The perception that most Black women desire to be curvy and voluptuous is a myth situated in the American imagination. In her book *Revolting Bodies? The Struggle to Redefine Fat Identity*, Kathleen LeBesco averred: "the possibility of passing, trying to lose weight, wanting to become 'normal,' is about the only recognized option available to fat women in twentieth century Anglo–American culture."[22] Since Black women are also citizens in an American society that abhors fat, it would make sense for them to work to attain slender bodies and have issues with weight. Oprah Winfrey's decades-long public struggle with her weight and her recent financial investment in Weight Watchers' stock, Roxane Gay's recent memoir that centers her issues with body size, Kerry Washington's admittance to battling bulimia, and Jennifer Hudson's commercially marketed, drastic weight loss are only a few examples of the stark reality about Black women and their bodies.[23] Many Black women wish to be thin. LeBesco also proffered that "Media aimed at African–American communities are increasingly reminding Black folk to pursue slenderness as heartily as their white peers do."[24] In addition Sandra Lee Bartky noted, "The strategy of much beauty-related advertising is to suggest to women that their bodies are deficient."[25] No wonder I have issues with my size, like so many other Black females. We too are consumers of mainstream advertisements that make us strive for a bodily perfection that is extremely hard or impossible to attain due to bodies altered by photo-editing programs. As a matter of fact, Bartky asserted "There is little evidence that women of color or working-class women are in general less committed to the incarnation of an ideal femininity than their more privileged sisters."[26] Similar to other cultures, representations of Black beauty are usually promoted by images of African–American waif models and celebrities in print magazines and commercial ads that endorse beauty products, supporting Bartky's claim that nearly all popular women's magazines feature dieting articles in every issue.[27]

In *The Embodiment of Disobedience: Fat Black Women's Unruly Political Bodies* and *Unbearable Weight: Feminism, Western Culture, and the Body*, authors Andrea Elizabeth Shaw and Susan Bordo, respectively, provide compelling arguments as to how and why the presence of the fat female body serves as a marker of direct resistance of Eurocentric standards.[28] However, I offer that the very existence of these types of arguments hinges partially on the truth about weight loss for virtually all women; that is, weight is extremely hard to lose. Thus, in America, fatness leaves women few options; try over and over again to lose the weight or learn to claim fatness as honorable and admirable.

But do we love our large bodies because we adore fat or do we love our large bodies because we cannot lose the weight?

In my case, I could not love the weight that categorized me in my eyes and in the eyes of mainstream America as ugly, disgusting, and asexual. I work to live in my honesty, and at this moment I lack the volition to re-embrace my fat body. Nonetheless, I revere Fat Studies advocates who are able to honor their largeness, and I am in the fight with them against size discrimination.

Fat Studies Advocate

Fat Studies constituencies advocate against the discrimination of fat people and promote size diversity. The Fat Studies field emerged to counter the argument of fatness as negative. The discipline, which reclaims the neutrality of the word "fat," grew out of the size acceptance movement of the late 60s.[29] Fat Studies scholar Marilyn Wann explained in *The Fat Studies Reader*, "There is nothing negative or rude in the word *fat* unless someone makes the effort to put it there; using the word *fat* as a descriptor (not a discriminator) can help dispel prejudice."[30] In addition, in an unpublished piece that she wrote for a Health Studies course Amy Farrell pointed out:

Unlike the medical and public policy studies outlining the "risk of overweight" and the "epidemic of obesity," the field of Fat Studies challenges us to think about the meaning of fatness, the power of fat stigma, and the dangers inherent when an apparent health crisis also becomes a moral crisis.[31]

The book *Fat Rights: Dilemmas of Difference and Personhood* by Anna Kirkland and the article "Human Rights Casualties from the 'War on Obesity'" by Lily O'Hara and Jane Gregg both highlight the need for America to end the vilification, harassment, and abjection of the fat body.[32] This period of disdain of the fat body is relatively new, as Gilman stated: "The obese, from at least the mid-nineteenth century on, were seen as a danger to themselves as well as to others."[33] He reminds us

each age, culture, and tradition has defined acceptable weight for itself, and yet all have a point beyond which excess weight is unacceptable, unhealthy, ugly, or corrupting. Today we call this "morbid obesity," and it is always seen as an issue of health.[34]

Even fat children are included in the vilification of largeness. For instance, a couple of years ago a billboard campaign emerged in Atlanta, Georgia, from Strong4Life[35] with pictures of fat children who appeared sad. The billboards said that chubby, chunky, and thick are still fat. Another billboard suggested that nothing is cute about fat if it leads to Type 2 diabetes. Yet another billboard offered that it's hard to be a little girl when you're not really little. I also heard on the radio that a legislator was trying to pass a bill that would remove fat children from their homes and place them in foster homes, arguing that because the children are fat they are being neglected by their parents. As one can see, the Fat Studies community is tackling a monster, but we are making advantageous strides in the scholarly and public arenas with several books published on the subject matter, the creation of Fat Studies college courses, several organizations chartered in the name of fat liberty, and the 2012 founding of "Fat Studies: An Interdisciplinary Journal of Body Weight and Society." Yet, even with this abundance of progress, Fat Studies scholars and advocates' textual and political reach has not yet proved significantly influential in the weight loss and health industries, and has not seemed to curtail America's obsession with being thin.

In my work, I am still developing respect and gratitude for both fat and thin cultures, identifying as a Fat Studies assimilationist and liberationist. LeBesco explains:

> A fat "assimilationist" works to secure tolerance for fat rights and experiences and tries to raise consciousness about fat oppression but still possibly conceives of fat as a problem ... a fat "liberationist" celebrates fatness and tries to secure for the fat a positively valued experience of difference from the norm; she or he recognizes fat as a problem only to the unenlightened and as a boon to fat people with "abundant" experiences.[36]

While LeBesco drew a clear distinction between the assimilationist and liberationist, I consider myself dually invested in both conversations. Though I'm no longer physically fat, I have experienced most of my life as a fat person and can relate to both the assimilationist and liberationist viewpoints. As a liberationist, I feel that fat should be celebrated and that losing fat shouldn't be positioned as the cure to all physical and social problems. As an assimilationist, I do believe being very fat can cause some health problems. For example, now that I am smaller my ankles rarely buckle and flip over as they used to do, and my cholesterol readings have been normal ever since the weight loss.

AUTOETHNOGRAPHY AND THE ARTIST

My cultural lineage in Blackness foregrounds my interest in and utilization of autoethnography. In addition, autoethnography proves to be a methodology that embraces interdisciplinarity, while simultaneously supporting critical aspects of my identity as an actress and artist whose work is steeped in activism.

When I survey and surveil my life as a Black woman and artist, one who descends from the plantations of the south by way of West Africa, and one trained in an acting methodology rooted in Afrocentricity, it seems that the function of autoethnography often parallels the endemic function and particularities of critical auto-narratives and storytelling in Black communities since their forced arrival in America. Black epistemologies and ontologies have been historically situated in and around the employment of orality; sharing carefully constructed narratives and tales, which served as sense making opportunities and liberatory modalities. Often, stories shared by enslaved

Blacks proved invaluable in that they critiqued the ruling establishment and simultaneously perpetuated ideologies of connection, celebration, and survival. Commenting on tales for strategic survival, E. Patrick Johnson wrote "Given the physical and psychological constraints of slave culture, the slaves mode of resistance manifested in the form of tales ... these tales provided temporary psychological relief from slave existence, but some forms of verbal double entendre afforded material results in the way of freedom."[37]

To be sure, storytelling in Black communities have always recognized the importance of honoring one's own voice, and the stories and voices of commonplace citizens. Acknowledging the historical value and honor bestowed upon common folks' narratives and voices in the Black community, Patricia Hill Collins points to this factor of recognition as a key feature of Black feminist thought. In terms of scholarly inquiry, she offered, "Many contemporary Black women intellectuals continue to draw on this tradition of using everyday actions and experiences in our theoretical work."[38] She further proffered, "lived experiences as a criterion for credibility frequently is invoked by U.S. Black women when making knowledge claims."[39] With this, when I was introduced to the current movement in the academic articulation of the historical practice of capturing and sharing critical auto-narratives, termed autoethnography, I immediately recognized and gravitated towards the value of the methodology because of my heritage.

In *The Ethnographic I* (2004), Carolyn Ellis defined autoethnography as "research, writing, story, and method that connect the autobiographical and personal to the cultural, social, and political."[40] In *Autoethnography* (2015), by Tony E. Adams, Stacy Holman Jones, and Ellis it has also been offered that autoethnography "emerged in response to concerns about colonialism,"[41] which echoes bell hooks' writing; "From times of slavery to the present day, the act of claiming voice, of asserting both one's right to speak as well as saying what one wants to say, has been a challenge to those forms of domestic colonization that seek to over-determine the speech of those who are exploited and/or oppressed."[42] Adams, Holman Jones, and Ellis further posit that autoethnography necessitates the recognition of "social difference and identity politics, an insistence on respecting research participants, and an acknowledgement of different ways of learning about culture."[43] Because of my lived experience in a marginalized body, from a young age, I have understood the importance of valuing difference and epistemological diversity. With this, autoethnography's *modus operandi* complements my imbued careful and critical mode of investigation of self and others.

13

Connecting diverse ways of knowledge building with the re-telling of lived experiences in the context of an autoethnography, Communications scholar Robin Boylorn stated that "[Black women's] unnamed theories and often unheard voices not only legitimate their experiences as sites of knowledge but privileges their sense-making capabilities for strategizing and analyzing their lives."[44] And like Boylorn, I have embraced the nuances and recent construction of Art Bochner and Ellis's "evocative storytelling," a framework coded in Black lineage. In conversation with Bochner and Ellis's evocative storytelling, described as "stories with raw and naked emotion that investigate life's messiness, including twists of fate and chance,"[45] storytelling of the Black tradition has already always been evocative, as they serve(d) as rich archives and salient (re)productions of reflexivity, connection, and critiques on life. A clear distinction of storytelling transmission, however, is that enslaved Black communities mostly shared knowledge orally because of a denial of basic human rights, while autoethnography cites writing as a central component. Yet even with this delineation, evocative narratives (now spoken and scribed) and its purpose are central writ large to both autoethnographers and *griots* in Black communities. Black women's or *blackgirls'*[46] work as critical autoethnographers evince the ways in which evocative storytelling still serve as essential modes of survival in the Black community, signaling Collins's reminder that "Even after substantial mastery of dominant epistemologies, many Black women scholars invoke our own lived experiences and those of other African–American women in selecting topics for investigation and methodologies used."[47]

Autoethnography is also my preferred methodology because it is expansive in that it allows one to traverse disciplines, and welcomes diverse ways of "getting at" the research. In *Autoethnography*, Adams, Holman Jones, and Ellis offer several reasons for doing autoethnography; "critique, make contributions to, and/or extend existing research and theory; to embrace vulnerability as a way to understand emotions and improve social life; to disrupt taboos, break silences; and reclaim lost and disregarded voices, and to make research accessible to multiple audiences."[48] Adding to this, I offer that I engage in autoethnography because by design the methodology allows researchers to substantially cross several disciplines. For me autoethnography significantly speaks to the multiple, diverse, dense particularities[49] and "thick peculiarities" of my Black female identity by welcoming the intersectionality and transdisciplinary situation of narratives. Hearing me refer to myself as having "thick peculiarities," Bryant Keith Alexander described "thick peculiarities" as "Indistinguishable and undiscernable variations in people and cultures that gives us pause. Not pause to speculate on their difference or their oddity, but to wonder in the diversity of our beautiful humanness; ripe with the variabilities of nature, time and place; affording space to move about in awe of others, while sustaining our unique ways of being in the world."[50] My addition to this is that referring to oneself as thickly peculiar in the context of autoethnography invites spectatorship, audiencing, and co-participation in one's lived experience with the understanding that the peculiarities hold rich possibilities to transmute and mirror back similarities discovered between self and other.

My thickly peculiar research is located within ethnography, while simultaneously opening up the work to other disciplines, invoking an "autoethnography with/in ..." framework. For instance, *YoungGiftedandFat: An Autoethnography of Size, Sexuality, and Privilege* (this book), and "YoungGiftedandFat" (the play), is autoethnography with/in Fat Studies, and with/in Theatre, and with/in Performance Studies, and with/in Black Studies, and with/in Black Feminist Studies, and with/in Sexuality Studies. Though my work is undoubtedly autoethnographic it is able to blur or sometimes erase disciplinary boundaries and public/private personas, intimating Joan Morgan's hip hop feminist theory of "fuckin' with the grays,"[51] as my work continues to bend and flex the imaginary boundaries of ethnographic disciplinary rootedness, which is always in flux as scholars continue to define new and ethical terrain in which to conduct our research.

By identifying autoethnography as expansive, I also mean that the methodology welcomes several ways of "getting at" complex narratives such as mine. Autoethnography allows one to utilize interviews, observations, recordings, performative embodiment practices, free-writes, and so forth, to help the researcher most effectively relay the information; knowledge that helps the culture tease through the personal and political affects, while honoring discord and unkempt, messy findings, which often implicate the self. Alexander comments on this implication as he offers "[the researcher is] *not telling stories about what other people did to them. They are telling on themselves in the context of culture*, as I believe that when I share stories of my own experiences—I am not a folklore hero but someone complicit in the politics of social and cultural happenings."[52] Alexander, like myself, values the risky nature of articulating subjectivity, vulnerability, and states of precarity that often surface in the researcher, who is at once telling her story and stories of others like her while employing various modes of inquiry.

Finally, autoethnography is a complementary research method for artists whose work is inextricably linked to activism, and the method is in conversation with actor training methodologies. In particular, my performance projects usually entail an activist framework, so the connection of the personal to the political and cultural in autoethnography supports the type of scholarship and performances I wish to produce as a Black woman and actress/activist. Both hooks and Humanities scholar Uri McMillan comment on the history of activism in Black women's performance work as hooks states that African–American performance has always been ensconced in liberation and activism,[53] while McMillan offers that "Black women's performance work has deftly and unapologetically embraced the feminist axiom "the personal is political."[54] Hence, with autoethnography often enacting and reanimating the politicized histories, structures, and formidable foundations of a particular subject matter or event, I found this method apropos to the central locus of my narrative.

Concommitantly, autoethnography proved a research friendly method to the artist in me, as the central form of data collected is often in narrative form, spoken or written. Data collected in narrative form is readily malleable for adaptation into a dramatic text because scripts are ultimately a compilation of stories. Further, the desire to extend my autoethnography into autoethnographic performance was quite natural for me because in addition to being a professor and scholar, I am also a serious actor and artist. By actor, I mean that I portray characters other than myself in stage plays and films; and by artist, I mean that I also write poetry, make artwork, write music, direct stage plays and films, and engage in performance art. In addition, I place high value on theatrical training, critiques of traditional theatre, and believe that performance should include aesthetic and professional qualities.

Autoethnography also has the ability to be in serious conversation with contemporary theatre making methodologies; of the stage and for actors. In *Bullied: Tales of Torment, Identity, and Youth*, Keith Berry pointed out "autoethnography enables scholars to creatively enact one-of-a-kind research that emphasizes openness and vulnerability from both autoethnographers and readers."[55] Heewon Chang emphasizes that autoethnography "enhances cultural understanding of self and others" and "has a potential to transform self and others" in *Autoethnography as Method*.[56] Here, I assert that some theatre methodologies, particularly those rooted in Afrocentricity,[57] have the aforementioned transformative and connective power. Take the Hendricks Method for example. The Hendricks Method, developed by African–American theatre director Freddie Hendricks, is an acting technique rooted in evocative storytelling on a stage, with the express purpose of devising material that invokes change and highlights social justice issues. And in this training methodology, though a performer can write her personal story, that story may be assigned to someone else to perform during the show. This possibility of power sharing in storytelling signals Omi Osun Joni L. Jones' ethnographic performance work, in which she allowed a member of the community that she was studying to play herself during the staging of a performance titled "Broken Circles."[58] In this way, autoethnography can operate similar to the way that theatre operates for an artist/activist who devises. Understanding performance artists/activists art making as a form of reflexivity, critique, and cultural connection, autoethnography provides the theoretical means and know how to further extend and critique politicized staged works in progress and displayed for public consumption. Theatre making and autoethnography also dually evince a connection with a culture, invites a relationship with an audience, includes scholarship and new contributions to expand research,[59] and puts "bodies on the line" with collective narratives being front row, center on a page or a stage, naked and dripping with the politic of being alone and not alone at once.[60]

Framing the Investigation

Articles written by Communications scholar Lesa Lockford and philosopher Cressida J. Heyes helped frame my investigation of the implications and performance of extreme weight loss.

"Social Drama in the Spectacle of Femininity: The Performance of Weight Loss in the Weight Watchers' Program" by Lesa Lockford provided a starting point to help me begin making sense of my ambiguity living in a smaller body.[61] Building upon Lesa Lockford's use of Victor Turner's social dramas theory as it relates to a weight loss support group, I also used Turner's theory as an entry-way to explore my *transweight* journey. As Turner posited, "the third phase [of social dramas], redress, reveals that 'determining' and 'fixing' are indeed processes, not permanent states or givens."[62] When I began my shake diet I was entering the phase of "redress" for what felt like the hundredth time (yo-yo dieting). It is in the phase of redress that I lost my obese body, while simultaneously maintaining my fat psychological existence and

17

developing a slender psyche. Eventually, it began to feel as if the "real me" oscillated in a liminal space between the fat me (Fat Sharrell) and the slender me (Slender Sharrell), creating a third me (Liminal Sharrell). The liminal space I am referencing is one in which my mind manifests in both a fat body psyche, a slender body psyche, and a mental unmarked space on a daily basis, often making me feel trapped. Though I've physically crossed a border, I am trapped by psychological borders, thus my reintegration or transformation is incomplete.

With this discovery I realized that I perform on various levels. My morbidly obese psyche performs as the slender person, and the slender person performs as the slender actress, and the actress performs the character. In Richard Schechner's familiar construction, I am not me (morbidly obese Sharrell), not not me (slender Sharrell), not not not me (slender actress), and then not not not not me (slender character). I constantly shift between liminal spaces. I am always in-between two entities and never feel as though I'm one integrated self.

In her 2006 article, "Foucault Goes to Weight Watchers," Cressida J. Heyes analyzed the extreme management and attempted mastery of the self enacted by Weight Watchers' members. Heyes pointed out discourse in Weight Watchers' pamphlets and testimonials that promotes management of the self, noting that weight loss programs create "docile" bodies by requiring them to be managed to the smallest details. A "docile" body is one that is under extreme scrutiny and control.[63] Though one may feel that she has gained freedom by losing weight, she is actually under more management than she was when she started her diet. This increased management is in line with Michel Foucault's belief that "the growth of possibilities occur in tandem with the intensification of power relations."[64] Similarly, Gilman expressed that "Dieting has become the means of self-liberation or of self-control and self-limitation. It is the process by which the individual claims control over her body and thus shows her ability to understand her role in society."[65]

When I lost this "unbearable weight" I suddenly placed more restrictions on myself, as also evinced by weight loss organization members. As a morbidly obese person, I lightly monitored my diet, but as a person that has lost weight, I specifically manage more details concerning my body. I now pay extreme attention to my hair, my dress, the way I speak, my food, my conversations, and my body fat. For instance, I weigh myself every morning. I go to the hairdresser more often than I used to. I also buy new clothes about once a month, whereas before I purchased new clothes about once a year. I constantly monitor what I'm eating and work to limit myself to two splurges per week on high sugar or high sodium foods. This type of monitoring is quite frustrating and is in line with Bartky's assertion that weight management tactics can cause the body to become one's enemy.[66]

★★★

July 4, 2002, Age 22
230 pounds
Dear Diary,

I begged my friends not to take me to the mall. I forgot why I hated malls and clubbing. Quickly, I remembered. Cuz these places are filled with girls I wanna look like. Sizes I'm not. Beauty I never see. Me, a plain Black big girl with a natural. I hate myself but I don't want to hate myself. I try to love myself but it's too hard. I try really hard. It's only natural for wanting the opposite sex to notice me.

Now I know why I hate malls and clubs and parties and socials. It's because I have to be reminded of what I'm not. I want to be thin and strikingly gorgeous. All the mall did was depress me. It has been depressing me for as long as I can remember. This is why I don't like going out at night. I am allergic to sugar and bread and meat and fat and all the things that I love. I am allergic. ALLERGIC. My day has been made a depressed one. I can't compete with women cause I don't like losing. I just stay home.

★★★

MY VERY FAT TREASURE CHEST

The textual data collected during this autoethnography included journaling, entries in my food diary, and diary entries from childhood to my young adult years. In my food diary I counted calories, set goals, and reflected on my levels of hunger. From age nine up until now, I have kept a diary that I regularly write in. Many of my diary entries focus on sex, men, and achievements. I include diary entries in various places to provide more context to either what preceded the entry or what follows the entry. Many diary entries signal my deep frustrations with being an ignored, invisible sexual being who, because of my fatness, could not fully pursue my desires.

My textual data also included "feel-notes" in place of field notes. Feel-notes are close siblings to field notes. In *Writing Ethnographic Fieldnotes*, Robert Emerson, Rachel Fretz, and Linda Shaw defined field notes as: "accounts *describing* experiences and observations the researcher has made while participating in an intense and involved manner."[67] While I could certainly use the term field notes, I have opted to employ the term feel-notes to describe the central information gathering tool used in my research. Feel-notes best describes the data collected during my intense exploration of my feelings and my body as a transweight actress. I further suggest feel-notes be employed in autoethnographic work that specifically engages with theatrically rehearsed performance, as taking field notes during the rehearsal and production process may prove difficult due to significantly long, uninterrupted spans of training, rehearsing, or performing, in which the full body is engaged. Feel-notes have to be collected soon after the event, whereas recalling events from childhood or many years ago does not constitute feel-notes. My feel-notes were taken before and after rehearsals, or directly after a very long event. They serve as internal guide posts that are (re)membered, revealing a sense of what happened to my body as I maneuvered in very different realms. To this effect, in this book the feel- notes are embedded within the text, and not visibly identified as such.

My non-literary textual data consists of photos and video recordings. I investigated footage of rehearsals and performances, my video diary, and pictures from both shows. To acquire the rehearsal and performance footage I utilized a small camcorder, often having my cast mates or peers record me. To maintain an objective lens (literally) and the secrecy of my study, they were told that I was researching my acting process. The video diaries consisted of me filming myself at home during the rehearsal and performance periods. With the help of a friend, I focused the camera against a wall and recorded entries in private throughout my research period.

The first show, *Holding Up the Sky*, was professionally videotaped, and portions of the second show, *Fences*, were videotaped by a graduate peer of mine. Both videos provide accurate representations of my slender body performing on the stage. Photographs for both shows were taken by a professional photography company and performers in the shows. Combined, these modes of documentation enabled an in-depth study through several lenses.

Six interviews were conducted during my autoethnography. I selected the interviewees based on their relationship with me while working on both shows. Interviews were integral to my study because they enabled me to access other vessels of knowledge and actively construct my experiences, while comparing my perceived reality with others.

I interviewed my mother, Beverly Luckett, because she shared a holistic view of my battle with weight on and off stage and she attended both shows. I interviewed Clyde Ruffin, the director of both plays; Willie Cogshell, the man who played my husband (Troy Maxson) in *Fences*; Chris Blackerby, the man who played my husband (Young Man) in *Holding Up the Sky*; and Milbre Burch, the playwright of *Holding Up the Sky*. I also interviewed a graduate female friend who does not wish to disclose her identity. Her pseudonym is April Waller. April attended both shows.[68] These interviews provided invaluable insight as to how my mother, artistic colleagues, and friend viewed me within my new body. Because I met the director, playwright, both male actors, and my female friend when I moved to Missouri, they were not initially familiar with my obese past. The director, playwright, and one of my stage love interests (Ruffin, Burch, Blackerby) did not learn of my past until I conducted the interviews, while I "came out" to Willie and April after knowing them for a few months.

I conducted my interviews with open-ended questions so that they would feel like casual conversations. In her book, *Narrative Analysis: Qualitative Research Methods*, sociologist Catherine Riessman stated, "Interviews are conversations in which both participants—teller and listener/questioner—develop meaning together, a stance requiring interview practices that give considerable freedom to both."[69] In *The Active Interview*, sociologists James Holstein and Jaber Gubrium remind us that all interviews are co-constructed. Co-construction means that knowledge is being made by both the interviewer and the interviewee during the interview.[70] Holstein and Gubrium asserted, "Ideally, the interview should be conducted in private. This helps assure that respondents will speak directly from their vessels of answers, not in response to the presence of others."[71] All but one of my interviews were conducted face to face in privacy, and the other was via e-mail. The face-to-face interviews were recorded and transcribed for repeated listening and interpretation. Riessman stated that "Close and repeated listenings, coupled with methodic transcribing, often leads to insights that in turn shape how we choose to represent an interview narrative in our text."[72] All of the interviews proved useful in my autoethnography and during the writing of my solo show borne out of the autoethnography.

I employ pseudonyms for most of the characters in this book to provide anonymity and confidentiality to all persons involved in my journey.

21

However, with permission, the real names of all the interviewees are used in the text and endnotes except for that of my female friend.

A Guide Through This Messy Text; or a Mess of a Tale

It's about to get messy
Just like life
Just like bodies
Just like my body
adorned with the residue of youth and struggle (stretchmarks)
Messy like a breakup that you didn't see coming
Messy like rain when the sun is out
Messy like nosebleeds and blurred vision
and summer days changing a tire
and icy days that welcome slips and falls
Bodies are always in a transitional mess
And we are always cleaning them up and fixing them
be it a shower or tending to a broken bone
It's about to get beautifully messy
like transweight bodies
Messy bodies that makes one remember the old you
but first squint before they acknowledge your transition: "you lost weight!"
And when the conversation is over they think to themselves
"she must be sick"
or if someone has gone from skinny to fat since high school
others say "damn she done got big"

Our minds are messy like that. We harbor thoughts that we rebuke, and can tell many tall tales. We can also be messily forgetful. And this mess, of course, can extend into our scholarship, a place where we are actually trying to unravel, (re)member, and/or critique the mess further. Indeed scholarship can and *should* be messy, especially the kinds of embodied research that engages human interactions. Bryant Keith Alexander notes, "[scholars] are mandated to get our hands dirty."[73] So as I dug into my mess of a life in order to capture evocative narratives, the text, of course, became a critical mosaic of new and old tales, poems, diary entries, interviews, photos, and critically reflexive thoughts.[74]

As a messy but coherent text, *YoungGiftedandFat: An Autoethnography of Size, Sexuality, and Privilege* strategically maps key events in my childhood, but focuses on the years 2008–2012, as this time span covers the period in which I went on a low-calorie diet and was invested in learning to perform slenderness on the stage and in real life as a new person.

The writing that follows this introductory chapter includes a dramatic shift in tone, as my scholarly voice makes way for a more nuanced colloquial voice. Yet at the same time, the colloquial voice should not be mistaken as less theoretical or even less sophisticated; the voice invokes a more organic telling of lived experienced; a voice that is uniquely mine. Understand that the telling of lived experience is always critical, and can always be told through diverse linguistic templates.

Chapter 1 operates in memoric narrative to help contextualize my youth journey through fathood. I recall childhood events to offer insight into how fatness became critical to my sense of self and sexuality, along with Blackness and femalehood. Chapters 2 and 3 outline my rapid weight loss experience and my experiences with performing in two plays with a new body. My experience with weight loss maintenance and the trauma of loss are addressed in Chapters 4 and 5, while Chapter 6 includes the script for my solo autoethnographic show, "YoungGiftedandFat." I include this performance script as an example of how to adapt an autoethnography for the stage, and to honor the possibilities and benefits of autoethnographic performance, especially when one is young, gifted, Black, and *fat*. To conclude, I offer a performative reflection in which I imagine an interview between a journalist and me 40 years after the release of this autoethnography.

> This text is messy
> Not messy as in an unkempt thing
> Not messy in the sense of being disorganized or confusing
> This text is messy
> it engages a range of styles and voices that are all distinctly mine
> modes of expression linked with my complex ever shifting
> changing
> fractured self
> that speaks to the whole of me

This project signals Norman Denzin's construction of messy texts as "[attempting] to reflexively map the multiple discourses that occur in a given social space." Citing G.E. Marcus' essay, "What comes (just) after 'Post'? The case of ethnography,"[75] Denzin also writes that messy texts are:

> texts that are aware of their own narrative apparatuses, that are sensitive to how reality is socially constructed, and that understanding that writing is a way of "framing" reality. Messy texts are many sited, intertexual, always open ended, and resistant to theoretical holism, but always committed to cultural criticism.[76]

He then refers to these types of texts as being "multivoiced."[77] In other words, this autoethnography is messy in that it is multilayered, and diversely dimensional. In some places I engage an Afrocentric cosmology of time—that resists a linear sequence and speaks to the operating features of experience that inform the telling of lived experience. These features involve flashbacks, flash forwards, snippets of memory, blurring boundaries between teller and audience, and bending time to interrogate both the past, present, and futures; providing the reader with all the available information that contextualizes meaning and invokes the happening.

At times the tales that I share may make some readers feel uncomfortable. The stories of living are not always pretty. They are not always neat, and they do not always have happy endings. This text does not endeavor to tell the reader how to think or feel or even unpack every entry. However, the text does operate as a sort of theoretical think mine containing many fruitful sites and entry points to explore what it means to have a perceived negative weighted identity. I also add that messy texts have multi-temporal potential as they can open up potentiality for imagining many futures on the page, such as the performative offering found in Chapter 7. In this way messy texts operate as analytical tools to investigate projected phenomena, mirroring ways in which we make our lives in the world; lives that are not clean and in order, but chaotic, full of havoc, with glimpses of beauty, and the summoning of circularity and vast emotional range.

Finally, I included Talk "Fat" Sessions after Chapters 1, 3, and 5. These critically reflexive moments operate as interludes or textual intermediaries to help guide the reader from one period in my messy journey to another. Alexander states critical reflexivity "establishes a conscious level of knowing, of reflecting and critiquing experience, and our own levels of complicity both in the process of reflection (in/on the objects/places/spaces of reflection) and the ways in which we make sense of that reflection in public discourse."[78] In addition, Denzin asserts: "[self reflexivity] refuses to impose meaning on the reader; the text becomes a place where multiple interpretive experiences occur."[79] In the reflexive Talk "Fat" Sessions, I reveal themes that stand out to me and discuss issues that are most pressing in that moment. As I read and re(read) the text to offer a meta-critique upon the forces and occurrences that have shaped my present being, I highlight the ways in which I attempt to stay in connection with myself, others and the world.

Teetering on the brink of insanity (sleepless nights, stress, thoughts of dropping out of plays, crying spells), while walking a fine line between the world as my oyster or food as my ointment to soothe my scathing, open wounds, I "write my life" for you ... and me.

NOTES

1 Solo performance artist Misty DeBerry made this statement at the Mellon/ Northwestern University Institute of Feminist Solo Performance in the summer of 2011.

2 Tracking the nine years from 2008.

3 Sander Gilman, *Fat: A Cultural History of Obesity* (Cambridge: Polity Press, 2008), 9.

4 Steven N. Blair and I-Min Lee, "Weight Loss and Risk of Mortality," in *Handbook of Obesity*, ed. George A. Bray, W. P. T. James, and Claude Bouchard (New York: Marcel Dekker, 1998), 805–818.

5 Susie Orbach, *Fat Is a Feminist Issue* (London: Arrow Books, 1978). Rose Weitz, "The Politics of Appearance," in *The Politics of Women's Bodies*, ed. Rose Weitz (New York: Oxford University Press, 2003).

6 Sandra Lee Bartky, "Foucault, Femininity, and the Modernization of Patriarchal Power," in *The Politics of Women's Bodies: Sexuality, Appearance, and Behavior*, ed. Rose Weitz (New York: Oxford University Press, 2003), 39.

7 Bartky, "Foucault, Femininity, and the Modernization of Patriarchal Power," 33–34.

8 Gilman, *Fat: A Cultural History of Obesity*, 13.

9 Francine Grodstein et al., "Three-Year Follow-Up of Participants in a Commercial Weight-Loss Program. Can You Keep It Off?" *Archives of Internal Medicine* 156, no.12 (1996): 1302–1306.

10 For a thorough list of recent and influential books, essays, and journal articles about or relating to autoethnography please see chapter 6, "Resources for Doing and Writing Autoethnography," and pages 139–140 (endnotes 88 & 89) in *Autoethnography* by Tony E. Adams, Stacy Holman Jones, and Carolyn Ellis. (New York: Oxford University Press, 2015).

11 In this book, I define slender as being in one's BMI (Body Mass Index) normal range or lower overweight range.

12 Patricia Hill Collins, *Black Feminist Thought: Knowledge, Consciousness, and the Politics of Empowerment* (New York: Routledge, 2000), 11–13.

13 I consider a short amount of time being six months to a year.

14 Hortense Spillers, "Mama's Baby, Papa's Maybe: An American Grammar Book," *Diacritics* 17, no.2 (1987): 64–81.

15 Clair Ellen Van Ens, "The Poetics of Excess: Images of Large Women on Stage and Screen" (dissertation, University of Texas at Austin, 1999).

16 For more information about the Hendricks Method, please see: Sharrell D. Luckett and Tia M. Shaffer, "The Hendricks Method," in *Black Acting Methods: Critical Approaches*, ed. Sharrell D. Luckett with Tia M. Shaffer (New York: Routledge, 2017), 19–36.

17 Freddie Hendricks made this suggestion many times while training actors, and during formal and informal interviews conducted with him over the past few years. For further reading please see Constantine Stanislavski, *An Actor Prepares*. New York: Routledge, 2003; Sanford Meisner and Dennis Longwell. *Sanford Meisner on Acting*. New York: Vintage Press, 1987; Uta Hagen, *Respect for Acting*. New York: Macmillan, 1973.

18 Uta Hagen, *Respect for Acting* (New York: Macmillan, 1973), 22.

19 Performance Studies scholar Bryant Keith Alexander made this statement at the Mellon/Northwestern University Institute of Feminist Solo Performance in the summer of 2011.

20 Judith Butler, "Embodied Identity in de Beauvoirs *The Second Sex*," paper presented at the American Philosophical Association, 1985, qtd. in Sandra L. Bartky 2003, 27.

21 Uri McMillan, *Embodied Avatars: Genealogies of Black Feminist Art and Performance* (New York: NYU Press, 2015). Mireille Miller-Young, *A Taste for Brown Sugar: Black Women in Pornography* (Durham, Duke University Press, 2014). E. Patrick Johnson and Ramón Rivera-Servera, ed. *solo/black/woman: Scripts, Interviews, and Essays* (Evanston: Northwestern University Press, 2013). Nicole Fleetwood, *Troubling Vision: Performance, Visuality, and Blackness* (Chicago: University of Chicago Press, 2011). Harvey Young, *Embodying Black Experience: Stillness, Critical Memory, and the Black Body* (Ann Arbor: University of Michigan Press, 2010).

22 Kathleen LeBesco, *Revolting Bodies? The Struggle to Redefine Fat Identity* (Boston: University of Massachusetts Press, 2004), 62.

23 Nathan Bomey, "Oprah buys 10% of Weight Watchers, stock soars," *USA Today*, October 19, 2015, http://www.usatoday.com/story/money/2015/10/19/oprah-winfrey- weight-watchers/74206132.html. Roxane Gay, *Hunger: A Memoir of (My) Body* (New York: HarperCollins, 2017). Charlotte Triggs, "Kerry Washington: From Heartbreak to Happiness," *People*, November 6, 2013, http://www.people.com/celeb-rity/kerry-washington-from-heartbreak-to-happiness.html. Jennifer Hudson, *I Got This: How I Changed My Ways and Lost What Weighed Me Down* (New York: Dutton, 2012).

24 LeBesco, *Revolting Bodies?*, 61–62.

25 Bartky, "Foucault, Femininity, and the Modernization of Patriarchal Power," 33.

26 Ibid., 34.

27 Ibid., 28.

28 Andrea Elizabeth Shaw, *The Embodiment of Disobedience: Fat Black Women's Unruly Political Bodies* (Oxford: Lexington Books, 2006). Susan Bordo, *Unbearable Weight:*

Feminism, Western Culture, and the Body (Los Angeles: University of California Press, 1993).

29 Sondra Solovay and Esther Rothblum, "Introduction," In *The Fat Studies Reader*, ed. Esther Rothblum and Sondra Solovay (New York: NYU Press, 2009), 3–4.

30 Marilyn Wann, "Foreword-Fat Studies: An Invitation to Revolution" In *The Fat Studies Reader*, ed. Esther Rothblum and Sondra Solovay (New York: NYU Press, 2009), xii.

31 This quote was pulled from an essay written by Amy Farrell in 2010. The essay was unpublished, but was found online in 2011 because Farrell wrote it for her Introduction to Health Studies course at Dickinson College and posted it for the course. I was able to track down the source of this quote through correspondence with Amy Farrell.

32 Anna Kirkland, *Fat Rights: Dilemmas of Difference and Personhood* (New York: NYU Press, 2008). Lily O'Hara and Jane Gregg, "Human Rights Casualties from the 'War on Obesity': Why Focusing on Body Weight Is Inconsistent with a Human Rights Approach to Health," *Fat Studies: An Interdisciplinary Journal of Body Weight & Society* 1, no.1 (2012): 32–46.

33 Gilman, *Fat: A Cultural History of Obesity*, 4.

34 Ibid., 3.

35 "Children's Healthcare of Atlanta Launched Strong4Life, A Wellness Movement Designed to Ignite Societal Change and Reverse the Epidemic of Childhood Obesity and Its Associated Diseases in Georgia." Retrieved from www.strong4life.com

36 LeBesco, *Revolting Bodies?*, 42.

37 E. Patrick Johnson, "Black Performance Studies: Genealogies, Politics, Futures" in *The Sage Handbook of Performance Studies*, ed. D. Soyini Madison and Judith Hamera (Thousand Oaks: Sage Publications, 2006). 452–453.

38 Collins, *Black Feminist Thought*, 37.

39 Ibid., 276.

40 Carolyn Ellis, *The Ethnographic I: A Methodological Novel About Autoethnography* (New York: AltaMira Press, 2004), xix.

41 Tony E. Adams, Stacy Holman Jones, and Carolyn Ellis, *Autoethnography* (New York: Oxford University Press, 2015), 21.

42 bell hooks, "Performance Practice as a Site of Opposition," in *Let's Get It On: The Politics of Black Performance*, ed. Catherine Ugwu (London: Bay Press, 1995), 212.

43 Adams, Holman Jones, and Ellis, *Autoethnography*, 21–22.

44 Robin M. Boylorn, *Sweetwater: Black Women and Narratives of Resilience* (New York: Peter Lang Publishing, 2013), 7.

45 Arthur P. Bochner and Carolyn Ellis, *Evocative Autoethnography: Writing Lives and Telling Stories* (New York: Routledge, 2016), 10.

46 See Robin M. Boylorn's construction of "blackgirl" autoethnography in "On Being at Home with Myself: Blackgirl Autoethnography as Research Praxis," by Robin M. Boylorn in the *International Review of Qualitative Research* 9, no.1 (2016): 44–58. Also see Dominique C. Hill, "Blackgirl, One Word: Necessary Transgressions in the Name of Imagining Black Girlhood," *Cultural Studies <-> Critical Methodologies* (2016): 1–9.

47 Collins, *Black Feminist Thought*, 276.

48 Adams, Holman Jones, and Ellis, *Autoethnography,* 36.

49 S. P. Mohanty, "Us and Them: On the Philosophical Bases of Political Criticism," *Yale Journal of Criticism* 2, no.2 (1989): 1–31.

50 Bryant Keith Alexander offered this definition during correspondence about the constructions of G. A. Yep's thick(er) intersectionalities and Satya P. Mohanty's dense particularities. Yep G. A. "Toward thick(er) intersectionalities: Theorizing, research-ing, and activating the complexities of communication and identities." In *Globalizing Intercultural Communication: A Reader,* edited by K. Sorrells and S. Sekimoto, 86–94. Los Angeles: SAGE, 2016.

51 Joan Morgan, *When Chickenheads Come Home to Roost: A Hip-Hop Feminist Breaks It Down* (New York, Simon & Schuster, 1999), 59. For further discussion of Hip- Hop Feminist Theory see Treva B. Lindsey, "Let Me Blow Your Mind: Hip Hop Feminist Futures in Theory and Praxis," in *Urban Education* 50, no.1 (2015): 52–77.

52 Bryant Keith Alexander, "Teaching Autoethnography and Autoethnographic Pedagogy," in *Handbook of Autoethnography,* ed. Stacy Holman Jones, Tony E. Adams, and Carolyn Ellis (Walnut Creek: Left Coast Press, 2013), 551.

53 hooks, "Performance Practice as a Site of Opposition," 211–212.

54 McMillan, *Embodied Avatars,* 5.

55 Keith Berry, *Bullied: Tales of Torment, Identity, and Youth* (New York: Routledge, 2016), 21.

56 Heewon Chang, *Autoethnography As Method* (Walnut Creek: Left Coast Press, 2008), 52.

57 Sharrell D. Luckett with Tia M. Shaffer, ed. *Black Acting Methods: Critical Approaches* (New York: Routledge, 2017).

58 Joni L. Jones, "The Self as Other: Creating the Role of Joni The Ethnographer for *Broken Circles,*" *Text and Performance Quarterly* 16, no.2 (1996): 131–145. (Author's name is now Omi Osun Joni L. Jones.)

59 Stacy Holman Jones, Adams, and Ellis, *Handbook of Autoethnography,* 22–25.

60 E. Patrick Johnson and Ramón Rivera-Servera, *solo/black/woman*: scripts, inter-views, and essays (Evanston: Northwestern University Press, 2014), xvii.

61 Lesa Lockford, "Social Drama in the Spectacle of Femininity: The Performance of Weight Loss in the Weight Watchers' Program," *Women's Studies in Communication* 19, no.3 (1996): 291–312.

62 Victor Turner, *From Ritual to Theatre: The Human Seriousness of Play* (New York: Performing Arts Journal Publications, 1982), 77.

63 Cressida J. Heyes, "Foucault Goes to Weight Watchers," *Hypatia* 21, no.2 (2006): 126–149). For further discussion of docile bodies (ready to accept control or instruc-tion) see Heyes' article.

64 This Foucault quote is found in Heyes' article, "Foucault Goes to Weight Watchers" on page 126.

65 Gilman, *Fat: A Cultural History of Obesity,* 6.

66 Sandra Lee Bartky, *Femininity and Domination: Studies in the Phenomenology of Oppression* (New York: Routledge, 1990).

67 Robert M. Emerson, Rachel Fretz and Linda Shaw, *Writing Ethnographic Fieldnotes* (Chicago: University of Chicago Press, 1995), 4–5.

68 Beverly Luckett, July 7, 2011; Clyde Ruffin, June 29, 2011; Willie Cogshell, June 18, 2011; Christopher Blackerby, June 2011; Milbre Burch, June 16, 2011; April Waller [pseud.] June 16, 2011. All of these interviews were conducted by Sharrell Luckett. Material from the playwright's interview (Milbre Burch) does not appear in this book.

69 Catherine Kohler Riessman, *Narrative Analysis: Qualitative Research Methods Series* 30 (Newbury Park: Sage, 1993), 55.

70 James A. Holstein and Jaber F. Gubrium, *The Active Interview: Qualitative Research Methods Series* 37 (Thousand Oaks: Sage, 1995), 4.

71 Holstein and Gubrium, *The Active Interview*, 11.

72 Riessman, *Narrative Analysis*, 60.

73 Bryant Keith Alexander, *Performing Black Masculinity: Race, Culture, & Queer Identity* (Lanham: AltaMira Press, 2006), 134.

74 To preserve the "original voice" and authenticity of my diary entries, I have chosen to include all misspellings and grammatical errors.

75 G. E. Marcus, "What comes (just) after post"? The case of ethnography in *The Handbook of Qualitative Research*, ed. N. K. Denzin and Y. S. Lincoln (Thousand Oaks: Sage, 1994). 567.

76 Norman Denzin, *Interpretive Ethnography: Ethnographic Practices for the 21st Century* (Thousand Oaks: Sage, 1997), 224.

77 Denzin, 225.

78 Alexander, xviii.

79 Ibid., 225.

Chapter 1

TOUCHED

The skin on my little brown knock-kneed legs was stinging. Kyree's itty-bitty 5-year-old penis was peeking out of the top of his red shorts. He had aimed his "ding-a-ling" and grinned as his warm pee shot across my body like water from a shower head jet streamer. I smiled.

I don't know if my mama saw him peeing on me from the kitchen window or if she knew something was terribly wrong when she saw my wide, shocked eyes and frigid stance as she walked into the backyard. I just know that directly after Kyree's act she yanked me up and threw me in a bathtub full of suds and water. I imagine that my mama yelled at him and sent him home after scolding him, or called his mother on the phone explaining to her why she just whooped Kyree's ass unapologetically.

Mama's big light hands rubbed the rag over my body. The "birds and the bees" speech began, but mama was much too late.

As she wrapped the towel around my small 5-year-old frame, I focused on her heart-shaped red lips and black drawn-on eyebrows. It was habitual for mama to don a full face of make-up with or without occasion.

"Mama, can Kyree come back over to play?" I placed my little dark brown hand on her large shoulder as she lifted me out of the tub and onto the cream hexagon-tile floor.

"No!"

"Can he come back later?"

"Sharrell, you betta leave me alone gal!"

Before we exited the bathroom she looked into my deep-set eyes. A mirror reflection. Somehow she knew I had already been "touched." But what could she do? The culprit was a child, just like me.

This was not the first time I had laid eyes on Kyree's ding-a-ling: probably the 15th.

Kyree taught me about young love before the TV could; made sure that I knew all the pleasure places on my body.

We stood behind a big oak tree in my backyard, which was full of unraked leaves from several summers' past. His little hand in my Rainbow Brite panties, while my giggles filled the air. Anybody else would have thought the laughter was coming from some happy little Black girl playing with Barbie dolls, but that laughter was coming from a budding sex-pot, full, bursting, and learning to be touched by a man.

I had already mastered touching myself.

The earliest age I can remember masturbating is around 4 years old. Big Bird and friends were painted on the burgundy brick nursery school located in a suburb of Atlanta, GA. Ham and cheese sandwiches, stank-breath teachers, and booger-nosed classmates made up my day.

I lay flat on my belly on the bright blue cot, and my fat-cheeked face was turned to the right. I pulled my right hand under my body and placed it directly on the part of my pants that covered my private parts. I took my left hand and positioned it parallel to my right hand. My thumbs touched as I started to move my hands, pushing on my vagina and then lightly releasing over and over. The pleasure pulsated through my body and I began to breathe harder as my butt rose to the shape of a high mountain and relaxed, continuously. It was nap time in my nursery school and I was taking full advantage of the restful hour.

"Aaaaaaah, Sharrell!" exhorted Mrs. Ringgold. She ran over to me. My left hand was jolted from under me.

Up off the cot my little body flew. Mrs. Ringgold was flustered and embarrassed. She sat me in a small chair.

"Sit right here and don't move!" She dared not look me in my eyes.

My dangling feet and toes stiffened. She had interrupted my orgasm and my body was reeling from the effects.

"Keep your hands in your lap where I can see them!" she exclaimed.

About an hour later, my father arrived to pick me up, and my lanky 8-year-old brother was tagging along. Jay had a long Jheri curl. I believed my mom secretly wanted him to be a girl. With big white buck teeth that faced one another, he wasn't a looker. He found me sitting alone in the chair and glided over to me.

"Ooooh you in trouble. What you do?"

I made my naturally mean face even meaner and shot him a threatening glance. "Nothing." But I wasn't sure that I'd done nothing. I had to have done something because Mrs. Ringgold had been watching me closely ever since nap time, hands included.

My father set his 6'2" frame in the comfy front office chair. My elbow rested on his strong knee. He still had on his navy blue work pants and his General Motors shirt. My brother stood in the corner of the nursery office not saying a word.

"Sharrell," big-lipped Ringgold cleared her dried throat. She leaned closer to my little heart-shaped face. Her breath smelled like roasted duck. "Sharrell, who taught you what you were doing today?"

My body was trembling.

She demanded an answer. "Sharrell, where did you learn to …"

My father interrupted with his husky baritone voice. "Aye girl, tell her where you got that from!"

I began thinking as hard as my little mind could. But no one came to mind.

My petrified gaze rested on the only person in the room who wasn't interrogating me. The person in the room who would, for years to come, catch me on the living room sofa with my baby hair edges sopping wet from the sweat that emitted while I was "booty-kicking," as he called it.

"Sharrell!" Mrs. Ringgold was yelling.

My index finger raised as I indicted my big brother for teaching me how to masturbate.

August 21, 1990, Age 10
Dear Diary,

Today I am so desperate I just wish I had a big butt and dick and muscular chest. I don't want him to stick it in me but I do want him to rub my chest, kiss my nipples, and squeeze my butt. I want to fuck this boy named Richard Beasley. I wish he could just stick his big juicy dick in me and make me scream. I wonder if that will ever happen. I wish it would. I hope he will be the one to end my viginality and I hope I will be the one to end his and all I have to say is I WISH I COULD FUCK SO BAD.

ALL YOU CAN EAT

Mondays were made for meatloaf smothered in red paste coupled with banana pudding.

The next day was reserved for Chinese food from up the street. Four large pails of greasy pepper steak and sweetened chicken with fried rice, while fortune cookies told of futures yet to unfold.

On "hump day" we'd fight over the leftovers from other nights. My big brother winning, little sister whining, all eyes on my mother to provide more fine dining.

McDonald's it was. Two double cheeseburgers and a supersized fry washed down with a Hi-C orange drink.

Thursdays were reserved for baked chicken wings. Dead washed meat lay in an oval spotted black turkey pan. Drenched in seasoned salt and garlic salt and salt and salt and pepper and more salt. Drooling over the barbecue sauce that bubbled while the wings were cooking in the oven. Forty chicken wings gone in one fell swoop as the family of five descended on the dinner.

And oh boyee! Fridays was Pizza night! After scarfing down four slices of six cheese pizza, we rushed to put up the rest of our share to be devoured on Saturday morning.

Then McDonald's for lunch and dinner and everything in between.

And if I woke up early enough on Sundays, the gift for going to church was McDonald's for breakfast, and the reward after church was McDonald's for lunch followed by a hearty home-cooked meal.

TATTED UP

In the fifth grade I had a crush on Antonio Wilson. He was skinny. His caramel complexion shone like the sun on his freckled face. He had a smile that melted my heart and he sat right across from me in the back of the classroom. I was located in that area because of my bad temper. He was seated there because he was a loner, or maybe because he was really shy. Either way, I didn't mind a little eye candy.

After my usual day of crushing on Antonio ended, I hurried home to find my father cleaning up; his normal behavior. My relationship with my father was one filled with short words and reverence. We shared the same fingers, ass, and anger. He had a temper out of this world, but he was rarely physical. I always say that the only thing that saved me from being a physical abuser is the fact that my family rarely made physical contact when we were upset. We would argue with each other from here to Texas, but we didn't hit each other.

My father was known as "Hey." My mama and daddy never took the time to teach my brother and me that our father's name was "Daddy," so we affectionately called him what she called him. We passed this tradition on to my sister when she arrived into the world 5 years after me. When I had friends over, I never tried to hide the fact that we didn't call him Daddy.

"Hey, did you eat all the popcorn?"

From the next room, "What?"

"Did you eat all the popcorn?" After a few seconds of him not responding, I would slam the kitchen cabinets.

Louder. "Hey! Are these pig feet in this pot?"

"Yeah, but leave them alone."

When I would sit back down in the living room next to whichever friend I was entertaining, the slow question would emerge: "Ya'll call him "Hey?" That's weird."

Highly defensive, "No it's not. That's his name!"

Coupled with a large amount of weight gain in fifth grade, my breasts began to develop. This is when I started to feel like my father was ashamed of me because I was fat. I noticed that the women he and my brother complimented on television looked nothing like me. They were slim like my mother and had a well-defined shape. My protruding brown belly encompassed my entire upper body while my knock-kneed legs took me where I needed to go.

I'm not sure if my father and brother had a clue as to what their comments about other women were doing to my psyche, nevertheless, they were critical in forming my awful self-image.

I felt like my father disliked me because I didn't look like my mother and for that reason alone, I wanted to change.

While my father was cleaning in the kitchen, I took my book bag to my bedroom, and then headed into the living room to watch TV.

The living room was an open area with 70s dookie-green shag carpet. The brick fireplace was to my right and behind me was a large opening into the kitchen. This house solidified my parents' upper-middle-class status that they longed for in their younger years. My father was washing dishes at the sink on the other side of the kitchen. His back was turned. And directly behind him was our stove, which had a sort of awning. The stove controls were attached at the bottom of the top cabinets and then there was a wide space in which one could see into the living room to get a direct view of the television.

My mother believed that the living room should be lived in, and this is exactly what we did. We had three medium beige sofas that connected to make a large square. Jutting out from the sofa closest to the TV was a chaise lounge. In front of that was a hassock. The hassock could possibly fit two small people, but when I situated myself in the center of the hassock I took up the entire furniture piece.

There was an old, large broken television sitting on the floor, on top of which we placed our newer television. My favorite shows were set to come on any minute now. I had started to discover my love for the arts around fifth grade as well. The Disney channel had a show called *Kids Incorporated* that came on around 4 p.m. This show featured young teens that went to school together and then after school they performed as a band at a local hang-out spot. Following this show was the new *Mickey Mouse Club*. When watching these shows I would blast the volume and sing along.

My daddy talking from the kitchen. "Turn that TV down."

"It's not loud!"

He was standing at the sink in his classic 70s shiny silk-looking shirt with his too-tight black dress pants and black dress socks, even though it was 1990. The water coming from the kitchen sink got louder. I didn't speak to him when I came into the house and maybe that put him in a bad mood; either way, he was grumpy.

"Sharrell, turn that TV down!"

I was pretty much obedient when he asked me to do something because he rarely asked anything of me. So, I finally turned the TV down just a little bit. Once I was enthralled in my show, my sister started to bother me.

Now Jamia was beyond weird. She was made from a different batch of genes it seemed like. My older brother and I were fairly identical. We shared the same skin color and hair texture. He was just a little taller, of course, and had a fade. Jamia was light-skinned like my mother and talked in a high-pitch tone. She seemed too short for her age and had Asian slanted eyes. Her classmates often asked if she was mixed with Chinese and Black. She laughed at the dumbest things and tattled every second. She hated curse words and liked to play with all of my toys.

I promise I attempted to be a good sister, but five years was just too big of a gap to have any type of connection. Strange enough, when she was born, my name suddenly vanished. One would think it would be the opposite, but I became known as Jamia along with the real Jamia. I had to constantly remind my parents that my name was Sharrell. After awhile, I just stopped responding when they called me the wrong name.

While I sat on the hassock, my atypical sister had noticed my budding boobs and decided she was going to mess with mine since she didn't have any of her own. As my father continued to fervently wash the dishes Jamia approached the hassock and knocked me out of my trance. She grabbed my right boob.

"Jamia, stop it!"

She laughed really hard and my daddy quickly told us to keep it down. She came up to me again and then with both hands she grabbed my right boob and I pushed her down with my right arm.

As she hit the ground, her face was perplexed. Then her face turned from a small grin to realizing the agony she was experiencing. Jamia began crying really hard and loud. I called her gay a few times and then turned to continue watching my show.

I'm not sure if I heard my father's heavy footsteps pivot in the kitchen into a lunge that would surely make it a lengthy evening, but I did hear him grunt as he hurled my favorite plastic green mug with ladybugs on it at my sister and me.

It all happened so fast. The mug struck the lower TV and bounced off of it and onto the floor. That shut us up, and quick!

Jamia hurried off into her room and I sat quietly, surprised that my father threw a cup to silence us, but happy that it worked.

About 15 seconds passed before I started feeling a sensation on my upper left thigh. It was slightly itching. I reached my right hand over to scratch my thigh and that's when my hand slid all over my leg in streams of blood that were quietly seeping out of my head.

My thigh was dark red. I started screaming. "I'm bleeding! I'm bleeding!" I ran into my mother's bedroom that connected to her bathroom, leaving a trail of blood behind me.

Once in her bathroom, blood dripped onto her counters and drawers and into the sink. I had no idea why I was bleeding.

"What's wrong with you?" My daddy walked quickly into the bedroom.

"I don't know!" He then joined me in the large bathroom. I sensed he was scared. He put his heavy hands on my face and found the problem. The cup put a huge, gaping hole in the left side of my head. He pulled my wound further apart and I screamed. We both could see the white fatty tissue peeking out of my head in the mirror and were terrified together.

My daddy ran to find the only small-ass Band-Aid in the house and placed it over my wound. Of course, that didn't stop the bleeding, so he gave me a rag and told me to press it against the wound.

Now was my chance to tell on him. Yes, my father was like one of the kids when it came to matters of obedience.

I quickly dialed my mother's work number and caught her before she left the office. "Mama, my daddy cut me with a cup!"

"What?" She was livid.

"My daddy cut me with a cup. He threw a cup mama, and there's a hole in my head!"

"Sharrell, where are you?"

"I'm at home mama. Jamia was messing with me and I hit her and then my daddy threw a cup."

Click! She had hung up the phone.

As my father re-entered the bedroom, he knew what I had done and started to get ready for the wrath of my mother that came upon us maybe four times a year.

"I called my mama."

"What'd she say?"

"Nothing. Well, she said she'll look at it when she gets home." I left the bathroom after fiddling with the Band-Aid once more and went back to my television show. For some reason, the wound didn't hurt. The entire left side of my head was numb, but I mustered up a few tears just for the effect.

When my mother's Dodge Ram luxury van pulled up, I didn't wait for the ignition to cut off before I ran to the door and threw it open. She had a few grocery bags in her hand. As she entered the foyer, she dropped the bags and turned on the hall light.

"Let me see." She was clearly tired from a long day's work. When her hands touched my head, they were much gentler and more loving than my father's. She had the tender care that all children yearn for.

"Yeah, we gotta go the hospital. You need stitches."

"Hey! Why you hitting on these children?" Uh oh! My daddy quickly retreated to the dining room and sat quietly. He had no response.

I took my mama's hand and led her to the bloodbath in her bathroom, but my father had cleaned it up. Her bathroom was spick-and-span and all

I could do was swear that it had looked like a cow had been slaughtered in there just an hour ago.

On the way to the hospital, my mother informed me that I couldn't tell the nurses or doctor that my father did this. So we concocted a story that I was running and slipped on something and hit my head on the edge of the kitchen counter. I spit this lie out quite fast when the nurse entered the exam room.

"Sharrell, that's a nasty wound. What happened?"

Fast as hell. "I was running and hit my head on the counter."

Looking back and forth from me to my mama, the nurse wasn't buying the story and she prodded. "You fell?"

"Yes." I looked the nurse in the eyes, and was thinking, heffa don't mess up my family. The nurse had a concerned look on her face as she scanned my mother and me one last time.

I had to get a bunch of stitches in my head. I was excited about all the attention from my mom. She probably took me out for ice cream afterwards. I can't remember.

When I returned home, my father saw the black stitches sticking out the side of my head. He assured me that it was going to heal quickly. I didn't care. I just wanted to lie down. I could now feel the pain from the incident and my head was throbbing.

When I returned to school with a white patch on the left of my forehead after a few days of being absent, I was immediately the popular girl. I reported the same lie to my classmates and to my teacher.

The wound healed nicely, but left me with a permanent scar. I like to think of it as my father's stamp of love. I didn't need a tattoo parlor or many years of greeting cards.

SPOTTING KYREE

I was big, colorful, and nearly bald on the first day of seventh grade. I was accepted into the minority-to-majority program in the county, affording me the opportunity to be bused 50 minutes north of Atlanta to attend a majority white school. I was excited about the transition.

My mother bought me a bright orange Cross Colours jean suit. My hair was also chopped off in preparation for a Jheri curl.

When I looked in the mirror I saw a very black face, swollen cheeks, deep-set slanted eyes, a double chin, four rolls on my neck with 10 dark skin tag moles, three skin tag moles on my left cheek, and a few moles poking out around my mouth.

The boys at school quickly looked the other way as I walked down the hall. I would often bump into several smaller classmates during the change of classes. These bodily greetings were followed by many apologies: "Sorry." "Excuse me." "My bad." "Are you okay?" "Ooops."

Then I saw this skinny boy running down the hallway. It was Kyree! He had moved out of my neighborhood around fourth grade and I hadn't seen him since.

Excited. "Hey Kyree!"

He was playing "tag" with other girls in the hallway. He slowed down and looked at me. I watched him focus on me. I watched him look me up and down as his head tilted to the side like a confused puppy. I was so much bigger than him it was embarrassing.

"It's me. Sharrell." I grinned, and before I could get another word out, Kyree ran off, chasing after a small, long-haired high yellow girl. I must admit I was a bit jealous that some other girl was getting that good loving.

November 11, 1992, Age 12
Dear Diary,

I'm so horney. Last night I went trick or treating. Got some candy. I was Ms. Wanda. I am so confused. Last night after I went to get candy, I called Richard and he asked me to be his girlfriend. We ain't even seen each other. I said let's be friends for a little while longer. I did not sleep well last night. He talkin bout he gone be thinkin bout me. I am so crazy.

FATTY BACK

"OK everybody." I stood in front of my seventh grade classmates, white and Black. "I'm going to dance and I want you to say, 'go fatty-back, go fatty-back, go-fatty back.'"

I invited my classmates to make fun of the fat rolls on my back while teaching them the chant that my brother made when he taunted me at home for being fat.

"Go fatty-back, go fatty-back, go fatty-back." The class sang in unison and got louder as I started to dance. I smiled at my seventh-grade teacher who smiled back, recalling the conversation that we had a couple days earlier about me learning how to make new friends.

Little did I know that my grandiose personality made me a perfect choice for the school play. If I could be fun and comical, surely I would do well in *Rapunzel*.

In this version of *Rapunzel* a portion of the play took place in a beauty shop and I was cast as an ensemble actress who cuts her long hair.

I stood onstage in rehearsal as I read the lines aloud: "I love my new hair-cut. I feel 50 pounds lighter!"

I stared out at the roughly 300 seats that would be filled with students. I imagined the laughter and heckling that would ensue after I delivered that line. I could just hear them: "Yo fat ass ain't lost no weight." "50 pounds lighter, hahaha." "You still big!" "Go fatty-back, go!" And then the auditorium would burst into the chant, "Go fatty-back, go fatty-back, go fatty back!" But this time I wouldn't dance. Tears would well in my eyes as I forced a fake smile, but I wouldn't be able to hold them back. And the school would see me crying. They would see a fat human crying right before their eyes. They would wonder how my big self could cry, affirming the messages I had received about my fat body from an early age.

"You're too big to cry, Sharrell."—sixth grade teacher

"Fat girls marry fat men."—eighth grade friend

"You should wear flowing shirts and skirts to cover your body."—Mama

And when I got home that night after being royally teased, I would pray for death and hope to reincarnate as a skinny, beautiful girl with a nice smile and white teeth.

I left rehearsal and never returned.

The Boy Who Cried "Fat"

I looked up at the black cement driveway that led to the woods in the back of the house. There was a makeshift pathway that led to another street that connected to my street. Folks was so saddidy about trekking in their yards, but the street-way home on this late evening seemed too long of a walk and I was tired. The worst that could happen was some old biddy yelling at me about crossing through her backyard. At least I knew that a boy who rode my school bus lived in the house with the special pathway, so I took my chances. My pigeon-toed feet and too big 12-year-old legs were moving real fast to get me up the driveway, hoping I was running quick enough to dash into the woods in their backyard without being seen. And just as I approached the woods, a teenage boy yelled from the window, "Hey fat girl!" I stopped, and turned towards the house. "Fuck you!" My erect left middle finger supported my response.

"Fat ass. Stay there and I'ma come outside."

I couldn't see his face through the screen on the window. "So!"

"I have a gun. I dare you to stay." He sounded much older than me. I was looking intensely at the window and wondering if I should stand my ground or keep walking.

About one minute passed. I was afraid, but wasn't a punk. The thought of him coming outside to ridicule me further was unbearable. I imagined the same encounter for a smaller girl:

"Sexy thang. Stay there and I'ma come outside."

Giggling. "No, I'm supposed to be home by now."

"Damn, you fine. You got your period yet?"

Giggling harder. "No, you nasty. Why?"

After licking the window screen. "Cuz that mean you ready for a real man."

Cutting my flirtatious bedroom eyes and turning away from the window to head on the pathway home. He would yell out, "If you come around here again, we fucking."

"Fat ass," the boy yelled from the window as I snapped out of my daydream. "You think I'm playing, huh?"

"Fuck you!" I retorted, and hurried into the woods, escaping.

The next day at school, the teenage boy's cousin, my schoolmate, informed me that he was in the house during the verbal altercation. He said he was glad I left because his cousin really did have a gun.

Did that teenage boy really want to shoot me? Did my body make him that angry?

This incident seemed like it was the start of being rejected by what felt like every damn boy in the world.

BOY TROUBLE

My best friend Tandie was from Liberia. We were similar, but very different. She had gorgeous bowed legs, a nice-sized booty, and A-cup breasts. We shared secrets, pink bubble baths, and chocolate skin. With her odd-shaped nose positioned like a full teardrop, I imagined her to be much cuter than me.

I felt she thought of me as the ugly fat friend with no self-confidence. To me, she was everything I wanted to be, minus the nose and her Seventh Day Adventist religion.

Worship on Saturdays was torture, as I attended Saturday service with her on several occasions.

On this spring day heading into summer, we decided to scour the neighborhood, looking for nothing, chatting about what 12-year-old girls chat about: who likes who, who is forming a singing group, and what high school we want to attend.

In the distance we saw Tandie's brother, Mendee, who was hanging with other teenage boys from the neighborhood, all 16 or over. As we approached them, my breathing increased and I became unusually quiet. My shorts were probably pulled into my crotch from the walking. Thick legs lotioned. Face greasy. I tried to take on a cute stance when we joined them.

"Damn, Mendee, how old yo sister now?" Tandie flashed a smile and answered. "I'm 12."

Another boy spoke. "Mendee, she gone be fine as hell when she get older."

They glanced over at me. My eyes darted around, knowing a compliment wasn't in store. I just hoped they left me alone. Then one of them looked at Tandie with lust, and then at me with disgust, and then back at Tandie.

"Take your fat friend home and don't bring her back."

My heart sunk.

Tandie tried to be a good friend, a quality she had lost by high school. "Ya'll quit being mean." She looked over at my empty eyes.

Another boy chimed in, "Yeah, don't bring her back."

"C'mon Sharrell," Tandie said softly. As we walked in the opposite direction she reminded me not to pay stupid boys any mind. I assured her I was OK.

I knew that the boys were watching us walk away, gawking at Tandie's nice ass and probably making fun of my square, flat booty.

I would eventually tell Tandie how I wished I was her, in one of our many counseling sessions with her and my brother acting as therapists and me being the fat, Black girl who needed help.

July 20, 1992, Age 12
Dear Diary,

OK, Tandie introduced me to this named Dwayne. And I like talking to him over the phone, but he talks nasty to me sometimes. And one day my mom over heard him and she doesn't want me talking to him. So what if I want somebody to shove their dick up me so I can have a nice thrill. But noooo, I have to live with every one knowing about my sexual life. Shit I want a dick.

P.S. I wish my mom wouldn't care.

Fat Girl Roles/Rolls

Eighth grade was one of the better years in my pre-teen life. I was placed in an Anger Management program after cursing in class on several occasions. The program consisted of completing worksheets, eating at a fast food burger joint, and swimming after school.

Towards the end of middle school, I decided to try my hand at theatre again because the passion to perform was so great that I could not deny the arts any longer, even if I didn't like my fat.

Luckily, there was a performing arts high school near my home with a great drama program. When my mom and I went to their Open House event, the drama department performed a short excerpt from their spring show. Students who would eventually become my classmates and lifelong friends were jumping around on stage, dancing really fast, and displaying extreme agility.

I felt like I could not execute the movements because of my size and I also felt that the director wouldn't want to cast me in a show, but my mom insisted that I audition for the drama program. I did, and was accepted. So, in ninth grade, I started on the path that eventually led to a career in the performing arts as a fat actress.

★★★

Playin roles covered in rolls
Blubber cakes hangin from my head to the toes
Freshman, so fresh on dat underground railroad
Leading the enslaved to freedom
Skin like chocolate gold
Shoulders so wide
Boyfriends! I cried
But the rolls gave me roles that didn't comply
small girls play women who end up in the "big house."
An indefatigable Stepp Sister, fat we all were
Why not showgirls, why not her?
Her, little legs choking from the fish net
stockings

A black leotard showing the skin and bones

Can I show mines too?

No, cover me up!

Cover me in a windbreaker suit

To play Béla Károlyi

Cover me in standing, and laughing ovations

Cover me in a robe as an opera singer

Cover me with child, a fat expecting mother

To be

Square booty in a round hole

Don't bother me, I can't cope

Only fat girl in the play

Acting wasn't fun anymore so I hung my actor's hat in the closet

with my suicidal thoughts.

THE SCOOP

Janine came around the corner of the backstage area cheesing! We plopped down on a rectangular table in the wings of the theatre, legs swinging, ready to share secrets. She had big doe eyes and a smile full of gums. But she was awkwardly pretty in her own way and mysterious. She tossed her head to reposition her yarn braids out of her face.

"Sharrell, oh my God. It was so good!"

"Ya'll did *it*?"

"No, I told you I was a virgin."

"Would you please quit holding on to that lie." She was still insisting she was pure. A year older than me, at age 16, Janine was the new girl in the drama program and all the dudes wanted a piece of her, but the most popular one was given a chance.

I had the biggest crush on this popular boy Janine was fooling around with. He was so earthy with a pointy nose and ear-length dreadlocks. Equipped with the best acting chops in the program and a lean muscular physique to go along with it, he made my heart jump. Just a few months earlier, I took my chances on him.

"Good evening." He answered the phone like a teenage weirdo. Good evening? I thought. I had taken him up on his offer after acting class to call if I needed help with anything. A few minutes into the stale conversation I tried to appeal to his esoteric sense of self.

"I was thinking about the stars and space the other day, you know?

"Yeah, yeah, yeah." That's all he ever really said, now that I think about it. I tried to show him I was philosophically deep.

"Like, where do humans really come from? We're so complex. We have feet, fingers that move, eyes, breasts." I hoped he would start to think about me sexually if he hadn't already.

"Yeah, yeah, yeah, right."

"And we try to make sex so taboo, but it's not."

"Yeah."

"Can I tell you something?"

He started to sound disinterested. "Yeah, yeah."

"I kind of like you." Panicked, so I gave him a way out. "But I'm sure you talking to somebody."

"Yeah, yeah, yeah."

A few months later, Janine and I were in the wings of our high school theatre gossiping about my crush. She knew I liked him and I knew he liked her. Maybe that's why we became friends.

"Promise you won't tell nobody." Janine whispered.

"Who I'm gone tell?" A long pause. "You sucked his *thang*?"

"No! But we kissed a bunch and …," she dragged out the last bit, "… he ate me out." My mouth flew open, half in excitement and half in jealousy. I jumped up in dramatic fashion, arms waving in the air and running around the small space in the wings as if she had just done a perfect triple Lutz. I sounded like an injured mouse while holding my scream in. "Was it good?"

"He just threw me up on the kitchen counter, pushed my legs open, and went at it, like it was dinner."

"Dang." I hopped back on the table. "Ya'll goin' to 'go together'?" Janine shrugged her shoulders in uncertainty while I reveled in knowing what my crush had done over the weekend.

Cherry Poppin'

"Get yo sexy chocolate ass in my office!"

I stopped in my tracks. The walk from the gymnasium to the art room in the building was not long, but on my way I had to pass the front office. Startled, I turned my head to see if what I heard was make believe or if the Center Recreation director had really just flirted with me.

"You a sexy chocolate thick thang!"

Stephen stood at 6'4" and had light hazel eyes. He was a former college basketball player still holding on to his basketball physique. I tried not to appear nervous and excited. I was only looking for a summer job as a camp counselor in South Atlanta, not a summer fling.

At 20, fresh from my sophomore year in college, I was sure my cherry was covered in cob webs and dust. Maybe Stephen could tell I was a virgin by my asexual demeanor or maybe my fast gait gave my secret away. Either way, he must've sensed my fat girl vulnerability.

Stephen got up from his office desk wearing tan work slacks and a coach-like collared dark navy-blue shirt. Damn he was fine. Reminded me of my daddy, just lighter.

He grinned as his eyes searched my body.

I wished I had on something more sexy. I was sweaty, and probably funky from a long day's work with the 5- and 6-year-old age group. I wore loose knee-length black shorts with a large t-shirt and a bra that didn't hold my size D cup breasts well.

Besides myself. "You talking to me?"

"You gonna give me some pussy?" He asked boldly. Stephen was brash and confident, and that shit was sexy!

He was lucky too, because at my age, I felt I desperately needed to find somebody to give "it" away to.

Before him, this 19-year-old had tried to take my virginity when I was 14 but he wasn't gentle and the pain was unbearable. I found out he was still with his baby mama and we broke up. And my only other long-term boyfriend was an ex-convict whom I had met on the phone while he was still in jail. He was 29 and I was 15. We never had sex. I think he was too scared because of the statutory rape laws. And I hadn't met Robert yet.

In the small dating life I did have in my late teens, there was a trend that emerged; most of the men who acted interested in me were much older than me, mentally and literally. But the 22-year difference between Stephen and me was the biggest age gap thus far. Further, he acted as if my fat was appropriate for a woman.

I knew there was nothing emotional there and would never be, so he was the one I could give my virginity away to. He was the one that I didn't have to get attached to, give "it" up and then be angry when we broke up.

At 7 a.m. in the early fall of 2000, I was driving my newly purchased red Ford Escort from College Park, Georgia, to Lithonia, where Stephen lived.

He opened the front door. "You made it."

Shit nervous. "Is anybody else here?"

"No, come on in here girl."

I turned and looked at the houses in the neighborhood to see if anyone was outside. As somebody's garage across the street began to open, he pulled me in and closed the door. The house was well lived in making it clear that he shared the home with somebody, like a family; perhaps a wife, or maybe a girlfriend. But I shut those thoughts out of my head as he placed his big hands around my big body, and led me to a small bedroom.

He was gentle. Why does it take men so long to learn to be gentle? Once we were both naked from the waist down, he placed a white towel on the bed. Then he laid me down with my butt over the towel and climbed on top. I was so anxious that I couldn't focus on the moment. I just looked up at the ceiling and prayed to God that I could take the pain.

Kissing on my shoulders, then sucking on my titties; looking up at me and grinning. Down some more, under the navel, and then I got a little confident and guided him to my treasure trove of flowing juices and seemingly edible sweets.

Wet. "Stephen."

"You taste good. This why I like them young girls."

Wetter. Half giggling and moaning. "Oh, really?" Then I started to squirm, like I usually do, pushing away from him.

"Where you going girl"? We were suddenly face to face and I could feel his hand on his dick, guiding it towards the place that Kyree had lit on fire at the tender age of 5.

I guess he looked up and saw my eyes shut real tight, cuz he offered me his hand.

"Hold onto my index finger, and squeeze if it hurts."

A breath. "OK."

Intense pain. Squeezing his finger. More pain. Squeezing harder, silently telling God to let him in. Breathing. Intense pressure. Pain leaving. Squeezing. Eyes open. Him breathing harder, as the pain turned to bearable pressure.

Thinking while he's slow humping: Is this sex? Is he all the way in me? I'm gonna miss my Geology test. Am I really doing *it*? Should I move my hips? What if …?

My thoughts were interrupted as he jumped up like lightning while icky, creamy wanna-be-babies dropped onto the white towel. Loud and intense.

"Shit. Fuuuuuu-uuuuck. Uhhhhhhhhhh." After a few seconds he looked over at me and saw me with my palms covering my mouth, holding back laughter. He plopped down on my body like a living fish that was just let off the hook. "That was good."

Eager and already in love. "Let's do it again."

UNATTRACTIVE

"OK. OK. Bye." Kelly sighed and looked over at me as she hung up her phone. We were seated in the small, nicely decorated living room of her one-bedroom apartment. My sneaker-clad feet were propped up on her coffee table. Trying not to let her see my eyes filling with water, I stared straight ahead looking at the TV that was on mute. "Well ..." Her voice trailed off as I interrupted.

"It's bad?"

Kelly nodded yes.

"What did he say?" I finally gave her a puppy dog look. I could tell she was trying to deliver his message without hurting my feelings. I shouldn't have put her in that position anyway.

"He just said he's not really attracted to you in that way."

"Did he say why?"

"No. He just said he's not feeling you like that."

"Fuck him then!" I didn't really mean it.

By my early 20s I was used to men not liking me. When I was younger they would be honest and tell me they didn't like me because I was fat, but as I grew older, the men began to seem more sensitive, so they just told me they didn't like me. Because I had a few crushes on men whom I shared large social circles with, I knew some of the women they had either dated or had sexual encounters with. I recognized a commonality in dating with most of those men; they only messed around with slim women.

A woman can be ugly or mean as hell, but if she is slim, her dating pool is much larger than a fat woman's dating pool.

OUT OF NOWHERE

Because I believed men weren't attracted to me, I began letting my guard down around them. I didn't bother to flirt or adorn myself with jewelry and cute clothes.

College brought the promise of studying more theatre. As a junior at Georgia State University I decided to audition for one-act plays staged by students in the directing class. After my audition, I was told to meet Robert, a student director, at the back of the theatre.

Damn he's short, I thought. And looks like a serious nerd with his big glasses and skinny frame.

"Hey." Robert had a deep-ass voice.

"Hi." Guard down.

"Yeah, I want you to play a part in my play. Can I get your schedule?"

During the rehearsal period, I discovered that Robert was also a writer for the school newspaper. Now this trait was attractive. And his quiet demeanor made me especially curious about him.

The performance came and went and shortly afterwards I decided to call Robert, not because I had a crush, but more so because I didn't understand how someone could be so quiet in person but so prolific on paper.

On the phone I would insist: "Robert, I know you got something to talk about because I read your stories."

"Ummm." He would then emit a laugh of confusion as to why I was trying to make him have a conversation.

I learned he was seven years older than me. I eventually invited him to a play and afterwards decided that he was too weird and quiet to befriend. A few months passed of not talking to one another, then one day he called.

"Hello." I tried to sound cute, not knowing who it was. We didn't have Caller ID yet.

"Hey."

Surprised that Robert called. "Who is this?" I pretended not to recognize the voice.

"This Robert."

Calm and collected. "Oh, hey."

After a few more awkward encounters that turned into dates, we began having sex.

After a weekend of intense sex and philosophical discussions about hip hop, I sped home in my red Escort, fed up with Robert and his uncertainty about being with me. I picked up my cell phone and dialed him. When he picked up, I was forceful. "Robert. I can't do this anymore. I'm tired of being your fuck buddy and nothing else."

"Dude, what are you talking about? Why we gotta put labels on stuff?"

Insistent! "Either you 'go with me' or don't call me anymore, and I mean it." I held the phone and listened to him breathe for a second.

Finally, he spoke. "Man, you right. OK. OK. Sharrell, will you be my girlfriend? Geesh."

Robert and I endured a six-year "on again and off again" relationship full of arguments and make-up sex. Through it all, I never imagined him to be attracted to me, even though he often called me pretty.

March 15, 2006, Age 26
Dear Diary,

I think it's coming to the point that I'm gonna kill myself. I was thinking about death and how I believe in reincarnation. Sometimes I feel like a failure. I wanna see a psychologist, but I need more. Why am I so afraid of being sexy and gorgeous? I have…when Lord am I gonna find happiness and love. I eat like there is no tomorrow … food … a comforter, etc. Love = hassle. No pain, no gain. 26 years in the making.

I'LL CRY IF I WANT TO

I sat on my apple-red couch and faintly smiled as my friends finished the "Happy Birthday" song. Reggie sipped red fruit punch, while J.C. ate a piece of my marble cake topped with cream cheese icing. My best friend Tyra was in the corner flirting with Reggie's cousin. And my two Cockapoos ran up and down my brand new townhome steps, almost as if they were moving in sync to the new Outkast song that was playing on the radio.

"Everybody. Can I have your attention please?" My good friend Jeff got everyone to stop the chatter. "Sharrell has shared some information with me and I think we need to listen."

Tyra, with her wide face and buck eyes, looked my way with a smirk. Other friends came out of the galley kitchen and gathered where I was sitting. Folks bit their lips, sipped on the cheap alcohol, and tried to appear invested.

"I'm not happy," I murmured as I ran my hand up and down the arm of the couch.

"Sharrell, what are you talking about …"

I cut Tyra off. "I'm not happy. I know I have a brand new home, but I'm depressed."

"Awe babe." Jeff rubbed my arm.

"Sometimes I think about ending it all. It's like I want to be here, but then I don't."

Tyra laughed lightly and whispered to J.C., "I just came to eat some cake." Others reminded me that I should be grateful for another year, and that I had so much to be thankful for. On and on they went. I retreated to my bedroom upstairs as my birthday party continued downstairs. Sitting on my bed, staring at the wall, I prayed to God to take my pain away, and decided not to throw any more public pity parties.

Thanks for Noticing Me

Tyra made her usual Friday night phone call.

Weary. "Hello."

Chanting and beat boxing in between words, "You ready? You ready? Let's go. Let's Go. It's Fridaaaaaaay. Ready to partaaaaaaay!"

I just sat quietly on the phone waiting for the hip hop madness to stop.

"Hello? Sharrell?"

"I'm here."

"C'mon man."

"Where?"

"There's this new spot on Peters Street. Gonna be a lot of men there. Ladies in free before 11 p.m."

"I don't feel like going." I told Tyra I would call her right back. At this point in my life I could best be compared to Eeyore, the depressed donkey from the *Winnie the Pooh* chronicles. His mantra: "Thanks for noticing me."

The phone rang after 20 mintues. It was Tyra. As I lay in the bed looking at my lavendar wall, I decided not to pick up. Years and years of failed dieting had brought me to the realization that I was going to be fat all of my life and I was getting bigger every few months. I curled up in my comfy bed adorned with red wine sheets and a mélange of blood-colored hues while I winced and made believe I was suddenly skinny. I would do this at least twice a day in hopes that my body would magically shrink.

While I fixed my eyes on my thick wrists for comfort, I felt a heavy weight in the middle of my body, causing my chest to collapse into black sorrow and currents. Salty rivers rolled down my face. I had mastered crying in silence. These nightly rituals usually subsided when I had to pee. The weight of the world caused a weak bladder.

When Tyra called back the third time, I picked up. She insisted that I put on some clothes and come out of the house. "Boys will look at you!" she assured me.

"Fine." I yelled into the phone.

"Cool. I will call you when I'm leaving."

I grabbed the only jeans that made me happy. They were regular blue with a little white washing on the front. They fit me snug and made my thighs look a little smaller. I found a simple black top with an oversized neck area. Black had become the color of all my tops. After applying my makeup I placed a fake nose ring on my right nostril. It was the perfect addition to my outfit. Jeans zipped, boots on, hair pulled back, bathroom lights out, cell phone charged; it was time to leave.

As I zoomed past my bed, I decided to take one last approving look at myself in the mirror. I quickly pivoted around, smiled, and stared at myself. I looked hot, like all fat people looked to me: hot and swollen and greasy and sad. I attempted to maintain my smile but my lips quickly turned into a frown. My eyes glossed up and the nose ring looked more like a piece of glitter stuck on my face.

As my cell phone rang over and over again, I thought of how heartbroken Tyra was going to be if I canceled. I picked up the phone. "I'm not going."

Tyra's tone elevated, "Why?"

"Because I don't like my outfit and I'm sleepy." We ended the conversation and I undressed in hopes that I was never invited out again.

March 28, 2007
Dear Diary,

It feels like you have something very special but nobody wants it. The soul hurting is a terrible feeling and that feeling produces tears. I cry alone at night. I console myself and rub my arm. I tell myself it's going to be allright. I marvel at my body. My big belly and weird looking boobs and fat thighs. I swear I'm beautiful. Do I like pain? Depression is such a constant visitor. This new guy tries not to hurt my feelings. He says we don't have sexual spark. Of course, why would I think we would? I never have that with anyone. I'm newsexual ... or nonsexual ... or diesexual ... or wastesexual ... or uglysexual ... or just sad.

ADMIRER

I hopped off my mama's lap, all of six years old, and chased my brother. He had just tried to plant a live granddaddy longleg spider in my hair. Through laughter I could hear my daddy basking in what he imagined was a very social future for me.

"Sharrell's gonna be fine," my father proclaimed while inviting a gaze upon my little body from all his friends and family whom he had invited to the summer cookout in our oversized, lush, green backyard.

"Mama, Jay won't let me catch him!"

"Come here Sharrell. Let mama get a picture." The smell of smoked pork chops on the big silver grill filled the air. I furrowed my face and climbed back in my mama's lap.

My daddy continued. "Look at her strong arms and legs. She gonna be a track star or a dancer. Wooooo-weeeeee. She's gonna have hips like 'this.'" My daddy used his hands to draw a womanly shape in the air. He came over and knuckled my face, making me laugh. "Kiiiiiiiiid." He bellowed with pride. "Yeah, she gonna be a heartbreaker, a homewrecker."

After the picture, I hopped out of my mama's lap as my brother approached her to ask if he could have a soda. I punched his leg as hard as I could.

"She got em!" My proud daddy exclaimed.

Figure 1.1: Sharrell, the early years.

SAY IT AIN'T SO ...
DADDY ISSUES?

Talk "Fat" Session

My father always seemed peripheral in my upbringing, but clearly he was not.

My favorite photo as proof of my father being in my life is at my 5th birthday party. I am sitting on his lap. This was my mother's doing. She was good at pretending. And we engaged in the performance with her. My daddy and I made it look like we knew each other; like this close behavior was normal, but it wasn't. Or was it? My daddy appears in many photographs throughout my life. His two-dimensional presence allows me to say he was there, and he was there too and he was there too, and there too—as I look in the real and imagined photo gallery of my life. A man who seemed emotionally unavailable in my life, in the same house, was everywhere but nowhere at once. These photos of my father and me often illicit a sincere smile, followed by a thought of "I guess he was trying."

If anything at all, my father taught me that men hurt women; real bad. And because of his teachings I worked to protect what I understood as my female power. I kept my power in "giving away" my virginity, no? I kept my power by telling on my daddy when he sliced my head open. I kept my power by throwing knives and scissors at my brother when he angered me. I kept my power by cursing at adults, chewing with my mouth open, and telling wives that I *knew* their husbands. I wait for no marriage, no boyfriend, no prospects, no professions of love. I call the "lover shots" or I think I do. I understood the pain women bring upon themselves and the pain men bring unto women, and I opted out.

How do we keep the mess of men and boys out of young girls' lives? They can fuck us up; and once we realize how bad we've been scorned, abused, or terrorized, it seems like it's too late. We look up and we are damn near 50 working out our daddy issues in whatever modes and methods are available to us.

My daddy, or my resistance to my daddy, had to be what compelled me to try a new diet, to really believe that I was going to give up food for months on end. Who else has that much power to make someone want to lose herself?

I felt like and still feel that my fat body was my daddy's dream unfulfilled. And when he began to get older and fade away, I suppose I felt an extreme urgency to fade away too; trying to be the perfect daughter before he left me for good. Maybe I thought that my shedding weight would help him see me.

I reflect upon the power of men in the lives of women. Why do we engage in these destructive size-changing activities over and over again? Has to be daddy issues, right? We are hungry, we are fatigued, we want the brownies, we want the salads with the fatty dressing, we want the desserts, we want the milkshakes, the meat, the salt, the sugar, the chocolate, and we want our fathers.

Perhaps I rebelled in the name of loss. A cleansing. A starvation. Transformation as punishment. Starvation as freedom. Transformation as connection. Starvation as redemption; a radical act of self-care. Transweight. Perhaps.

Reader's Reflection #1

Take a moment and reflect on how you see yourself, and draw that image below. Don't forget the side view.

CHAPTER 2

DISAPPEARING ACTS

June of 2008, Age 28
264.5 pounds

I arrived at the Excel Bariatric Center in an attempt to right what had been wrong my entire life. I felt like the shake diet was my last option and I had nothing else to lose. The wooden chair was wide enough to hold my ample thighs. As I squeezed into the space directly above the chair pad, I was hoping for a miracle with the 800-calorie diet that loomed ahead for the next 16 weeks.

The beige walls resembled any other medical office. The receptionists wore mosaic-swirly-dark-blue-and-white ascots, complemented with a navy blazer and white blouse. It was quiet. I was surrounded by other big bodies that I assumed would be my weight loss cohort.

As I sifted through the pages of the usual waiting room magazines, my mind was blank. I had no further opinions about whether or not I should try this low-calorie diet and risk further humiliation from my family and friends if I failed. I was here because I needed to be in order to survive in this backwards world. I neither wanted to stay or to go, so I just sat there and let life take the lead.

Moments later, I was whisked away to begin my enrollment. I stood in a long hallway. The nurse pointed in the direction of the scale at the other end of the hallway and said she would be with me momentarily. At this point, I wished I had access to a sort of "last meal." Walking down that hallway was akin to being on death row.

The scale was unlike any I had seen before. The weighing contraption was big enough to hold six people at once, but I had to be weighed alone. After the scale confirmed that I was morbidly obese, weighing in at close to 300 pounds, I was asked to stand in front of a blank wall so they could take a picture of me. This "before" picture stood for everything at that moment: for my sanity, for the many men that ignored me, for my morbidly obese aunts, for my hundreds of tear- filled nights, for my right to be thin, and for my father who I felt was ashamed of me.

★★★

Spring of 2007, 1½ Years Earlier

I don't think I ever told my father I loved him until he had a debilitating stroke. My big 20-something-year-old body shadowed his as he lay there looking up at me wide-eyed from his nursing home bed. I knew it was time to change his diaper but I wanted to do my usual "identity" check before I proceeded to care for him.

"Hey, who am I?" He glanced up at me and let out a chuckle showing space where his teeth once were. Then he answered, "Peaches."

Ever since he had "stroked out," he had been mistaking me for his sister Peaches. Peaches wasn't in the room and she damn near wasn't in his life anymore. I understood the confusion though. Peaches and I were both dark skinned and shared a big body.

I proceeded with my usual interrogations, locking eyes with my lost father. "Hey, I'm Sharrell."

He laughed in his horse-like tone and said, "You ain't Sharrell. Sharrell is a great big ole' woman. Got an ass from here to here." To illustrate this statement, he stretched out his arms as far as they could span from left to right to show the distance between one butt cheek to the other. I half way giggled and half way frowned.

After spending a few years in the nursing home, we were able to bring my daddy back home and care for him ourselves. My mother administered his medicine and took him to doctor appointments and I was responsible for his baths, always letting him wash his *thang*. And I think he appreciated that.

I would usually see him in the evenings when I stopped by before going to my house, but one particular morning I had to get something out of his bedroom for the play I was directing with my high school drama students. Well before 8 a.m. I tiptoed in his bedroom as not to disturb him. He was facing the window on the wall opposite his armoire that I needed access to. Once I retrieved what I came for, I contemplated whether or not to say hello to him. I have to get to school, I thought. I shouldn't wake him up, but I really wanted to say hello.

"Hey."

He didn't respond. "He is really sleeping hard today," I mumbled. Louder, "Hey!"

No response. Then I noticed he was super still. Gosh, he's in a deep sleep. Heart picking up the pace. Me trying to put the small, simple puzzle pieces together. In a quick, fearful reaction, I mustered up all my fat girl strength and punched him as hard as I could in his left arm. He didn't move. I then leaned over his body to look at his face, and there they were; eyes like glass, open, blank to the world. I ran to the hallway, careful not to enter my mother's room, but leaning through her doorway.

"Mama!"

Waking up and groggy. "What girl? You here?"

"Mama, my daddy not moving. He not moving. Call the ambulance." I was trying not to scare her, but there was no way around it.

She lifted her head up in disbelief. "What? What you mean he not moving?"

I walked back in the room with my daddy, but my mother didn't follow so I came back out of the room, and there she was standing, mind empty, in a daze. I dialed 9-1-1.

"Hello. What's your emergency?"

"Ummmmm … my daddy ain't breathing." The operator sounded really concerned, and she was talking fast to the dispatchers. Then she asked his age.

"72." I was sure of it because his birthday was coming up. Then everything slowed down, including the paramedics walking up our long, winding, big hill. He was pronounced dead on the scene.

Whispering to my mama while the paramedics, police officers, and one detective bustled about our large, rectangular living room, "You better cry."

I had seen too many police shows and I knew that we were suspects. Mama let out a big wail in the living room, as my cold daddy was leaving the house on the hill for the last time.

★★★

JUNE OF 2008

This "before" picture stood for everything at that moment: for my sanity, for the many men that ignored me, for my morbidly obese aunts, for my hundreds of tear- filled nights, for my right to be thin, and for my father who I felt was ashamed of me. Before the camera flashed at the Excel Bariatric Center I took a deep breath and let my stomach go. I wanted all the fat to be caught in time: my flabby arms, my pant- size-24 waist, my overly cushioned neck, and my surprisingly skinny ankles buckling under immense pressure.

I actually mustered up a smile in my purple sleeveless tank top and Lane Bryant short blue jeans.

And with the flash of the camera, the last known photo of me as a fat woman was taken.

DAY 1 OF THE DIET

July 5, 2008

I lay on the mauve microfiber couch. You could compare me to a whale that had come to shore to die. My right leg was elevated on the dusty brown coffee table. I was flailing and deprived, and it was only 12 p.m. My cabinets and refrigerator were empty. Shakes surrounded me, but I could only have one every 3 hours. I had already had two weight loss shakes and my next shake was scheduled for 2 p.m. I was ravenously hungry.

If I got off the couch and took a trip down to McDonald's it would be my regular routine.

My round dark face quenched up as my head bobbled from side to side with each hunger groan. My eyes were heavy from caloric depravation and I blinked slowly. The TV was off because I was concentrating intensely on not eating. The food commercials would surely send me into a binge and my whole life would be flushed down the toilet.

The doorbell rang. In walked my mother and sister. My mother was supposed to enroll in the weight loss program with me but reneged at the last minute because she admitted she wasn't ready to give up steak.

My sister was tagging along as usual, with her quirky slim self. She got the good genes, as they say.

As my mother approached me, a rectangular bright orange cardboard box appeared like magic in her left hand. The blue words scrawled on the box read "Diet Sunkist." I lifted my heavy head off the couch and told my mother to put the sodas into the fridge. My mother was doing her usual; trying to help me succeed.

I believed my mother had three McDonald's tender-grilled chicken sandwiches with extra mayonnaise and onions stashed away in her olive green minivan, and she would dash out and get them if I asked her to. But I had to practice strict discipline. I insisted on mastering the diet.

As I listened to my mother scurry in the kitchen to put a diet soda on ice, I knew she had sensed tears were about to flow.

"Sharrell, did you already have a shake?"

"Yeah, mama."

"Just one?"

"Two, mama."

"Well, when can you have another shake?" My mother passed me the cold glass full of diet soda. The room became quiet as I reported that my next shake wasn't scheduled until a whole 2 hours away.

My sister let out a high-pitched laugh and exhorted, "Mama, she's not gonna make it!" Usually at this moment, I would resort to name-calling, but I remained quiet because I feared my sister was right.

HAVE YOU SEEN HER?

July 18, 2008

Dear Diary,

It is day 14 of my low-calorie diet and I am still doing great. 251 pounds. I had a few cucumber slithers, but other than that, I've done well. I am working on focusing on the end result more. The days are going by faster and it is not as hard to maintain and I have stopped thinking about food as much. I had a dream that I ate three slices of pizza last night and drank some soda. Gosh, it was funny. This fast is helping me find a new me. Stay focused!

August 14, 2008

Dear Diary,

Today is a milestone! I have lost 30 pounds on the program. I weigh 234 pounds. Yippee. In this next phase, I am going to concentrate on my psychology. I am entering an area I can't remember being in. I don't want to get scared and move backwards, so I'm going to think really positive. I want to increase my exercising. Thanks God ... tell my daddy I said hello and to look at me now :-) love ya!

September 11, 2008
Dear Diary,

I am doing well. 217.5 pounds. I have been cheating off the wall and I think it is because it is period time. I have decided to wean myself off slowly, so today I had no chips and I started to read my daily inspirations again. I took some bites of this chili that my friend mistakenly left over my house. It just looked too good and I took me some bites. I also ate mini pretzels in the cabinet. God, grant me the will power to stay faithful.

September 26, 2008
Dear Diary,

Well ... all I can say is ... wow! I have lost a total of 53 pounds on the weight loss program. I am a little overwhelmed but I'm working through it, trying to stay focused and definitely motivated. This past week was a good week weight wise, but I am still eating ... yet, I promised myself I would always write it down, be truthful with myself. I don't recognize myself when I look in the mirror, and on some days I look taller. I am ready for the 2nd half of the roller coaster. I have 47 pounds to go ... yes, I'm headed for the "100 pounds lost" mark ... stay with me God.

SIZE 12

October 10, 2008
Dear Diary,

203.5 pounds. I declare! I never thought wearing a size 12 would be this much fun. I am soooo excited. I jumped up and down in the dressing room when I put on size 12 jeans. To make sure it wasn't luck, I got another brand of jeans and put on a size 12 in them as well. They fit too! I kinda lost my appetite these last few days ... still cheating, but not as much. My hormones are out of whack I think and I have noticed some minor hair loss. I am still running this course. My dream goal is to lose 100 pounds and I have 39 pounds to go. I feel like I can do it. I know I can. I just have to stay focused. Love ya!

October 17, 2008
Dear Diary,

204 pounds! What a bummer! I have been walking around moping for the past two days because of this half pound gain, but I can't act surprised. I have been eating like a pig at the last supper. I decided not to eat with my drama students during rehearsal to take the temptation away. I did ok yesterday, but broke down and ate a Healthy Choice meal and a piece of a pop tart. My scale at home says I weigh 200.2 pounds, roughly, but I am going to stick with what the Excel Bariatric Center scale said even though I was at the end of my period and bloated. I had a crummy day at the gym yesterday too, but it was good that I went and I had fun in the aerobics room. Love ya still … fat and all!

December 6, 2008
Dear Diary,

Well, I promised myself I would use my massage gift certificate that my students bought for me when I reach 185. I'm close. 186 pounds. Life has been a little hectic because I am trying to prepare my graduate school application. My friend introduced me to this Chinese restaurant that makes great vegetarian meals. Yesterday I crashed and bought two helpings of Chinese food. I ate some, froze some, and gave my friend the rest. I ain't even trying to eat the rest of that mess. I like healthier stuff. I really want to lose 100 pounds. I'm just tired of teaching high school. Pray for me God; that I stay steadfast and not turn to my old ways! Love ya!

February 13, 2009
Dear Diary,

181 pounds. Well, hello. Yesterday, I was notified that I received a Full Scholarship and a teaching assistantship to attain my Ph.D. in theatre at the University of Missouri, Columbia. I could hardly breathe and I was crying and everything. I went to my group session at Excel and that was good. I'm at a standstill as you see, but all is getting better. I'm actually looking forward to the future! Hey daddy! Love ya :-)

UPPERCUT

I remembered to call Robert, my ex, and touch base with him while in a clothing retail store. He and I hadn't talked much during my transformation for various reasons. I still admired his maturity and private manner.

Our relationship often felt closeted towards the end. Though I felt like he loved me, we didn't really parade our affection in public. I'm sure the fatness played a part in our decision to end the relationship.

I dialed his number, excited to tell him the news about going to grad school. I was also wearing his white Fruit of the Loom small-sized t-shirt. His was the first small size I can remember wearing. He had left his shirt over at my house months earlier, and it was the only thing that fit on the day that I found that I could no longer wear any of my large tops. White t-shirts in the size of small became my signature top because I knew I could wear them.

His phone rang. "Hello." He picked up in the daytime, which is rare. Something about his deep voice always relaxed me.

I stood in front of the department store mirror, looking at my new shape. Curves very unfamiliar.

"I have exciting news!"

"OK. OK." He tried to sound invested in the conversation. "Go ahead."

"I have on one of your t-shirts." I giggled.

"Sharrell quit playing. What is it now?"

"Alright. I was accepted into a Ph.D. program in Missouri!" I was smiling so hard, and giddy because I loved talking to him, especially because by this time I knew he had a girlfriend. Talking to him made me feel like I was making him cheat a little bit.

"That's great. That's great." I could tell he was smiling on the other end. He cleared his voice and eased into a transition. "I have some news too."

I looked in the mirror again, smiling and swaying a bit from side to side. "OK." Looking at myself looking back at me.

"I got engaged." Silence. More silence.

"Wow, Robert. Wow."

"Yeah, so we both have things to celebrate."

After several moments of uneasy breathing that was turning into a cry, I uttered, "Does she know you're a product of divorce? Several? Does she know that?"

He let out one of his, "you know me too well" laughs, while I watched my eyes get glossy and slowly fill with bitter sadness.

MISSING

IF YOU HAVE INFORMATION ABOUT SHARRELL LUCKETT
CALL THE ATLANTA POLICE DEPARTMENT AT 404-614-6544

Name: Sharrell Luckett
Missing From: Georgia
Date Missing: 7-5-2008
Date of Birth: 1-5-1980
Age: 28
Sex: Female
Height: 5'9"
Weight: 272 lbs.
Build: Heavy
Eyes: Dark Brown
Hair: Black, Natural
Race: African American
Complexion: Dark Brown

Clothing: (Dark jean shorts; purple
sleeveless top; yellow bracelet; light
gray head band, black Keds)

Body Markings:(two piercings in each
ear; skin tag moles on face; visible
stretch marks)

CIRCUMSTANCES

(Last seen in downtown Decatur
near Excel Bariatric Center & Starbucks)

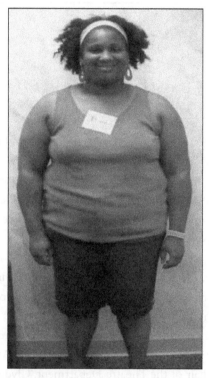

Figure 2.1: This flyer is a creative response from Sharrell that speaks to her epic
sense of loss after she lost weight.

CHAPTER 3

PASSING STRANGE

Soon after my physical transformation I packed up my life and headed west to start working on my Ph.D. in theatre at the University of Missouri.

My department was holding auditions for the world premiere of a play called *Holding Up the Sky*. This play has leading characters named the "Young Woman" and the "Young Man," who are wife and husband. The play also has several ensemble roles.

Because of my history of being cast in asexual, unfeminine roles as a fat actress, I was sure that I would be cast in the ensemble. I even perused the script focusing only on the ensemble roles, while ignoring the lines of the "Young Woman."

On the day of the auditions I wore basic black. When I walked into the room, seated at the table was the African–American director and then Chair of the Theatre Department, Clyde Ruffin, and other members of the design team.

★★★

Sharrell:	When you first met me was there any physical indication that you can think of that I used to be bigger?
Professor Ruffin / Director:	No. There would be no way for me to know that. I have to deal with what I see in front of me. I wouldn't look at you and say, "Oh I bet she used to be much bigger."

★★★

I was given a paragraph to read with intensity and dramatic flair. After doing my best, Professor Ruffin informed me that he wanted me to read for a certain part. When I received the script excerpt, I looked at the page and saw lines for the "Young Woman."

My heart started racing because surely he had made a mistake. I glanced up at the table and just as I was about to make sure that he had given me the right lines, he informed me that I was to go with Chris, the young man who eventually played my husband, and practice the lines.

★★★

Sharrell:	When you first met me was there any physical indication that you can think of that I used to be bigger?
Chris/"Young Man":	To be honest there wasn't. And I didn't think so even after getting to know you.

★★★

I was confused and anxious. In my mind I didn't fit the role. The "Young Woman" was supposed to be beautiful and believably desirable. When Chris and I found a small space outside of the audition room, I panicked.

Stressed. "I have no idea why he has me reading the lines."

Chris was high yellow, probably mixed. And though he was not my type he made good for some eye candy. He encouraged me, "You're good. You're perfect for the role and you should get it. Now let's run these lines."

I squinched my face and began to read the lines with him, but I couldn't stop thinking how wrong I was for the part because I wasn't feminine or beautiful. With quick thinking I decided to alter my voice a bit and tried to be dainty. I knew I had to control what I sensed was my big body, and I decided to pretend that I was Halle Berry because she was super feminine and pretty by American standards of beauty.

As Chris and I walked back into the room, I swayed my hips a bit and batted my eyes making what I thought was sexy, slow contact with the audition team. I also took my hair tie off of my waist length single braids so they could flow down my back during the scene. Managing to suppress my low self-confidence, I imagined myself to be thin while looking into Chris's eyes as we performed. I became determined to nail the part.

Later that week, I received an e-mail saying that I, Sharrell Luckett, had been cast as the "Young Woman." I leapt up and down in my living room and grabbed my cell phone. Mama was on speed dial. Before she could say "hello" I cut her off.

Chanting. "I'm the lead. I'm the lead. I'm the lead." I danced around the coffee table.

"When'd you find out?"

"Just now, I got an email."

"Oh good. When is the show Sharrell?"

"You gotta come see it. Mama, it's the lead character! And I got a husband. And mama he cute for real. I don't know if we kiss or not, but I think we do. I gotta read the script again."

"Oh. Okay. When is the show?"

Out of breath, "November I think." I was now standing still with my right big toe bent into a sickle shape pressing down on the carpet to make up for my different length legs. I sensed her silent thoughts.

"Mama, I'ma go to the gym. I just gotta go a lot."

"I didn't say nothing Sharrell."

"You proud of me?"

"I'm happy that you're happy Sharrell."

In His Eyes

Sharrell:	Before you met me tell me what you thought about the physicality that the "Young Woman" needed to possess.
Professor Ruffin/Director:	In my mind the "Young Woman" represented the first woman. What would the first woman have been like if I were the creator? From a design perspective, I wanted her to appear as if I could just reach down into the soil using my desire to create a woman, and just pull her up out of the earth. That's how I started. What would she be like? How would she present herself? How would she fit or place herself in the world. And so from a physical standpoint, there had to be something about her that reminded me of nature and

creation and the earth and all of that. In my mind, she needed to have some color, she needed to be able to move fluidly, because you know she's just been pulled, so she's fluid, you know. In the world I was creating she had to have some flesh on her. Yeah, I wouldn't wanna pull bones up outta the earth. Don't want no bones. I want something with some flesh on it, and to me there's nothing more sensual than a woman who has some weight but moves gracefully and with confidence. I was looking for that sense of body consciousness that says I'm comfortable in my own skin because I don't have anything to compare myself to because I'm the first woman so there is no judgment as to whether or not I'm worthy, unworthy, desirable, or undesirable. I'm fully confident because I'm the only one. I am. I'm here and I am woman. A woman who presents herself with no apologies and no judgments.

Sharrell: So, when you just described this young woman that you would pull out of the ground, physically, was I bigger than that, was I smaller than that?

Professor Ruffin/Director: No. You are just about right.

Sharrell: OK

Professor Ruffin/Director: If you were bigger, I probably would not have [cast you] … I'll say that.

RIGGING THE COSTUME

The costume rendering that was shown to the cast and me was that of a slender Black woman clothed in green and brown earth tones. The costume was beautiful, complete with waist wraps, head wraps, and bangles for the wrists and ankles. Professor Ruffin designed them. Gosh, he is talented. The character's stomach, legs, and arms were shown in the drawing. As we sat in the rehearsal room, it hit me; this costume rendering represented the director's vision of me, the actress portraying the "Young Woman," and she was slender with long legs, a flat stomach, and shapely exposed arms. Did I look like that? How am I going to tell him I'm really fat? I wanted to scream at the top of my lungs, "I'm not me!" But I wanted to play that role more. So I just sat and nodded quietly while conjuring up ways that I could alter the design so as to not reveal my "true" identity.

I began with the stomach. My extreme weight loss was unusual in that I have very few physical indicators that I used to be fat. I've been told that when people see my body with clothes on or in a bathing suit, they have no idea that I used to be bigger. I have stretch marks on my lower belly area, but my stomach is relatively flat; no "six pack" though. So, I figured that if I could tie a sash around the lower part of my abdomen, hiding the stretch marks, then I could let the top part of my torso show.

Because I've always been athletic, participating in track and field and basketball, the muscles in my legs were well trained. I wasn't too concerned about showing them. In fact, I was actually looking forward to the audience marveling at my toned, well-defined limbs.

But my arms tell a very different story than my stomach and legs. The flabby fat hanging very low from opposite the biceps beckons questions and curiosity about my physical past from onlookers.

I entered the well-organized office where African–American theatre books lined the shelves and African art adorned the walls.

"Professor Ruffin, you in here?"

In a deep commanding voice, "Yes."

"Professor Ruffin, you got a second?" I worked to make my face look calmer than usual.

"Sure, have a seat."

"Professor Ruffin, I have issues with my arms. I don't like showing them." Wanting the conversation to be over quickly. "I just won't feel sexy if I show them." The average height, stout Black man leaned back in his chair and focused his eyes trying not to look at my arms that were covered by long sleeves. I knew I was breaking a cardinal rule: don't complain about your costume if you don't have good reason. I really wanted to tell him that the show would go to hell in a hand basket if he didn't cover my arms. That I wouldn't be able to focus.

"Well, I'll see what I can do. Maybe I can cover them with some netting fabric."

Relieved. "That would work. I just have issues, you know." I thanked him again for his help and exited the office.

★★★

Sharrell:	What did you think when I came to you and asked that my arms be covered during the show?
Professor Ruffin/Director:	I had never even noticed your arms.
Sharrell:	What were your thoughts?
Professor Ruffin/Director:	I was like, she trippin'. I thought you was trippin' as a young woman being overly self-conscious about something that I didn't think mattered.

IRON FIST

"Whatever happens, I don't wanna hang with Mia tonight," my new friend April exclaimed as we prepared for an evening out at a Black fraternity party.

April and I met when we both arrived at the University of Missouri for our graduate studies. After discovering we lived on the same street, just a few duplexes down from one another, we began to study together, talk about the lack of Black men on campus, and support one another in our respective programs, hers being psychology.

We were trapped in the white, country Midwest with very few entertainment outlets for Black people. To our surprise, we found out some alumni of a Black fraternity on campus were throwing a party at a nearby convention center, and this was the perfect opportunity to be with our people, if only for a night.

I also enjoyed Mia's company, with her Bed-Stuy hood swag and many tattoos that covered her legs and arms. She was a single mom who was defeating the odds, and working on her master's in sociology.

Mia and I were about the same height, and she spoke her mind and cursed with conviction, like me. She also wore long-sleeved shirts with short-sleeved graphic shirts over them, like me. I admired her solid size 6 body, while I was wavering between a size 6 and 8.

I was the tie between Mia and April in grad school, but on this night April refused to carpool with Mia to the frat party. So April and I rode together, and Mia met us there.

After a few hours had passed at the party and several Long Islands later, someone decided that we should continue partying at the frat members' hotel.

I sat in the convention center lobby, looking cute, but stand-offish in my black-laced baby doll dress. I was slightly drunk. My wig for the evening was full, tightly coiled jet black ringlets that brushed my shoulders. Even after

I lost weight, I continued my habit of wearing wigs on occasion, simply because I liked them.

Mia, who met us at the party, showed off her caramel complexion legs by wearing a short peach-colored dress; April was in her usual conservative, dark a-line dress with short heels. There we were: all tipsy as hell.

"We're going to the hotel," the slurred words escaped April's mouth.

Damn! I shouldn't have had those Long Islands! I thought. Words were floating in my head. Fractured thoughts. Was we fucking the dudes? Were we getting naked? Are they pouring more drinks? Is anybody cute? I stumbled towards the exit door of the party.

There was a very light-skinned dude chatting it up with inebriated April. She gets all the dudes, I thought to myself.

"Sharrell, I'm gonna go with him. We're taking a taxi to my house." April's eyes tried to fixate on me behind her tan-colored glasses.

"A taxi? OK, cool. Can the taxi drop me off at my place?" Wait, that wasn't the right response. I concentrated harder to sift through my clouded thoughts. She's not supposed to go with him. I tried again.

"April, I'm going to come to your house with you and the dude."

She responded in her drunken stupor. "OK, great! I will fix breakfast and pancakes. You want coffee, Sharrell?"

"Dude, it's like 3 a.m., you're gonna fix breakfast?"

"Yes." She and the guy proceeded to exit the lobby through the turn-stile door.

Focus Sharrell. She's not supposed to go with this guy. You shouldn't go with him either. Focus.

I ran up to April and grabbed her arm. "Hey I'm a lil off, but ..." The yellow dude was getting furious. I was messing up his "cut" for the night. "I'm not sure what's the right thing to do, but I don't think I'm supposed to let you go with this boy to your house."

"But I want to go." April looked like a lost puppy.

"I know, but I'm supposed to be a good friend." Just then, slightly sober Mia interrupted. "We going to the hotel."

I was relieved. Tattling on April like we were in pre-school. "Mia, April is trying to go to the house with this dude and I don't think I'm supposed to let her go."

"Noooooooo," Mia said. "We are all going to the hotel together." The light- skinned dude walked away quietly, having lost his prey for the moment.

Loud noises, chatter, girls laughing in high heels and short skirts. Me in a short dress with heels. Dudes appearing thirsty. Grinning, still with alcohol in their hands. Did I sign up for an orgy? I had to set things straight.

I opened my mouth and shouted as loud as I could in the lobby of about 23 Black males and females. "Nobody's having sex!"

Silence. More silence. Blank stares. I had accused all of the girls of being hoes by mistake.

About 20 minutes later, April, Mia, myself, and two other girls were all cooped up in one car, headed to the hotel. As the alcohol began to wear off, we laughed. I laughed even harder because April ended up in the car with Mia after all.

We arrived at the Empire Suites, sitting in the small 4th floor lobby directly across from the elevators.

April and the light-skinned dude were at it again. She was sitting in a lobby chair and he was on one knee staring lustfully at her. Mia was somewhere "caking" with another guy, probably showing off her many tattoos. And I sat in a gray plush chair, alone.

As much as I tried to appear friendly, my "stay away" demeanor that I had developed as my fat girl defense shone through.

Whenever a man would compliment me, I'd muster a smile, and try to bat my eyes a little, but being around several men made me highly uncomfortable. I felt as though I was at the mercy of men to validate my beauty, and since I didn't want to be neglected, I chose not to mingle. I was perfecting my meanness, my brash personality, and my "stay the fuck away" attitude.

As the same yellow dude whispered shitty nothings in April's ear, he began to glance over at me to see if I was listening. I was. He was trying to get April to come to his room. She was still slightly drunk, fawning over him. A few more kisses on her ear and he would have her. But no sex parties were going down on my watch.

"Why don't you come to my room?" He softly suggested, while April fingered his chest.

"She's not going anywhere," I said firmly. The guy shot me a look full of anger. I continued. "She's staying right here."

"But what if I want to go, Sharrell?" April said as I rolled my eyes.

"April, you're not in your right mind."

The guy, on one knee, looked me squarely in my eye and projected his voice. "Why are you all in her business? All the other girls are with a man.

Look somewhere else. Find somebody who ..." He continued, but I didn't hear the rest.

My blood began to boil. He reminded me that I was alone at a party. Was he suggesting that no one wanted to talk to me? Was he calling my slender frame fat on the sly? Was he saying that men were ignoring me?

His words cut deep. Took me back to the many times that I was always alone in the club as a fat girl while my smaller friends, pretty and ugly, were getting 'hit on' by men. Took me back to a pain that stung, an anger that is often suppressed. His words took me back to my middle school years to a time where my fat rage leapt out whenever I was offended or hurt.

At 29 years old, my heart was racing. My fists became sweaty as my fingers began to tense. I quickly scanned the room. One lamp, two lamps, a fake tall plant and a glass table. All could be used as weapons. I was ready and willing to fight. Doctoral student and all, I was going to whoop his ass and this offense was worth going to jail for.

I began to mumble. "I can look where the fuck I want to." Louder. "I can look where the fuck I want to!" She was back, middle school Sharrell was back. I yelled at the top of my lungs at 3 a.m., voice shaking. "I look where the fuck I want to! You don't tell me what to do! Fuck you! Who the hell you think you talking to?"

I was provoking him. As soon as he lunged at me I would pick up the silver lamp directly to my right and bash his head in until blood drenched the walls. He would pay for every motherfucker's wrong doings.

I continued. "Lame ass bitch! Fuck you!" I stood up in my heels. Makeup still intact. So pretty, but so nasty. I was ready.

Other frat members who heard the commotion came running around the corner and wrapped their arms around him, urging him to go to his room.

I yelled some more. "You fucking asshole. I look where I want to. Bitch ass nigga!" I could feel hood Mia behind me, ready to strike in my defense if she had to.

The yellow boy who was about to get his ass beat retreated.

I was shaking. Eyes red and watery. The alcohol seemed to be out of my system. I looked around.

"Damn Sharrell." Mia sounded surprised.

April slurred. "Thank you, Sharrell. You are a true friend."

As the frat brothers tried to convince me to leave the lobby and come into their hotel room to calm down, I caught my reflection in the oval lobby mirror. The girl staring back was so gorgeous and so unfamiliar. Nostrils flared and eyes severe, I decided to sit down and gather myself. I wanted to go home.

Size 10

October 30, 2009
Dear Diary,

I'm lonely. I know I can throw one hell of a pity party and I feel one coming on. I'm tired of Missouri and I miss Black folk and people who look like me. I find myself calling boys that I don't really like. I just need somebody to care about me, ask how my day went, be invested in what I'm feeling. Someone to call me and just give a shit. Even prettier than ever at a size 10, Sharrell is still single with no prospects. Hopefully I will feel happier tomorrow, but right now, my love life sucks. I wish you could talk back to me.

Staging Sex

I was at dance rehearsal to learn choreography for the sex scene in *Holding Up the Sky*. Professor Ruffin wanted the sex on stage to be in the form of suggestive, provocative movement.

The outfit for this rehearsal consisted of black Lycra tights with cotton red "booty shorts" and a light gray top.

I looked down at Chris' face, strategically placed in-between my crotch by the choreographer. My right leg was bent over his shoulder while he kneeled, looking up at me. I liked this position.

As the choreographer looked at both Chris and me in this pose, I kept trying to hide how excited I was to be able to be sexy and feminine in rehearsal. Having a dude between my legs in public was finally justified. No one would question his desires for my body, even if it were make-believe.

We tried a few more positions and eventually came up with a dance that effectively and artistically insinuated sex onstage with an orgasm. The next day we performed the dance for Professor Ruffin and the entire cast:

> I sexily walked up to Chris as he threw his arms in the air, my hands rubbing over his bare nipples and abdomen. Fingers stretched, feeling the shaved parts of his body as I walked around him and caressed his entire bare back. As my hand passionately

rubbed across his neck, I completed the circle and stood directly in front of him, locking eyes.

Our elbows arched back and then we extended our arms out in forward motion to simulate a thrusting movement. First, my arms went over both of his shoulders while his arms extended past my waist. Then we switched arm positions. Up and down, our arms exchanged positions and we continued this common West African dance movement as we sped up, backs arching with each thrust. After about eight arm thrusts, I lifted my downstage leg and wrapped it around his waist to simulate an orgasm.

I could hear the cast members gasp.

Chris gripped my leg tightly, opened his mouth with glazed eyes and heavy breathing, while I arched my back until my head was upside down facing the floor. I began to glide down. Head, then upper back, lower back, and then he cascaded down with me, as we slid to the floor in a lying position. I added a full leg extension into the air as my long skirt completely fell to the floor, revealing the full glory of my beautiful, toned, dark cocoa leg.

"Stop" the stage manager bellowed. Chris quickly got up off me. The cast was quiet. I came out of the trance.

Professor Ruffin walked slowly to the stage, glasses close to his dark brown, bearded face. The director/preacher/full professor motioned for me to come closer.

I left my fellow actor's side and knelt down at the edge of the stage.

"I know what's missing," Professor Ruffin said.

My eyebrows raised as I listened for the instructions. We only had a few rehearsals left before the show opened.

"Sound."

The tension in my neck released as my head fell slowly forward and closer to the director.

"Sound? You want us to make noise?" Was the preacher really telling Chris and me to vocalize the sensuous touches and orgasm in the scene?"

"Yeah, we need sound." He spoke quickly, seeming almost embarrassed that he was even having the conversation. "Now, tell Chris."

Professor Ruffin had a way with words and he didn't seem to shy away from speaking his mind, but on this occasion I was instructed to tell Chris that we had to make sexual noises to complement our choreographed sex scene.

This is why I love acting, I thought. I can justifiably get away with moaning like a phonesex operator and parading as a pornographic superstar with an audience, fulfilling secret desires I've had for many years.

November 5, 2009, Age 29
Dear Diary,

Life has been going pretty good. My show opens next week and I'll be roughly 175 pounds. This is exciting! I am being lifted twice and I get to have an orgasm on stage with moaning. Gosh. I wish I could fuck him for real. It's so real on stage. We connect so well. My costume is cool too! I'm showing a lil bit of belly and a lot of leg. My mama is flying up Monday. I know she is going to laugh when she sees the sex scene. I haven't had sex in a minute. I'm hoping to score several times over Christmas break. Ha ha ha. I wish my daddy could see me. Maybe he can. Chris is a cutie pie. I pray that my husband is as beautiful as he is and smells just as good.

INTERVIEW WITH A FRIEND

Sharrell: Was the sex scene convincing for you?

April: I was convinced and I was like, oh, we are really caught up in the moment, like this is for real. This isn't just an intimate moment; they are really doing "it." Now I remember you talking about the sex scene and you were like, oh my God I have to pretend to have sex with this really gorgeous man and I was like great, fantastic. But you had anxiety about it and I kept thinking, what is she stressed about?

TEENY TINY

March 9, 2010
Dear Diary,

Hi!!! 170.6 pounds. It's been a while I know and yes, I've been eating heavily and exercising too. I am still pushing towards my 100 pounds lost mark, but I have learned that I can't rush the body and that I still enjoy food. So, my goal right now is to get out the 70s. I fluctuate every day and I know this because I weigh myself every morning no matter what. Sort of like facing the music. I have fought chocolate binges, pork chop binges, potato chip binges and I drink a bit more Starbucks now that I'm around it more. All in all, I will keep on the good fight. I know I can do it. Slow and steady wins the race. Love ya and thanks God!

FENCES AUDITIONS

The doors of the renovated church were huge and daunting. I could tell by the shiny texture of the brown paint and absence of dust that the doors had recently received a makeover, just like me. It was October and the gray door handle was frigid. Columbia, Missouri was offering up that crisp coolness that shocked me the year before. It's too early for this type of cold, I thought to myself, while wishing I was in the ATL soaking up that long ass summer that always extends into October.

At 175 pounds I stood in front of the doorway and prepared myself to enter. For this occasion I put on black eyeliner, penciled in my eyebrows, and used a sheer burgundy lip gloss. These auditions were important and light makeup always makes a world of difference.

I stood still in my usual pigeon-toed position and focused on my breathing. I had rehearsed my monologue earlier that morning, but knew I couldn't deliver it if I was a nervous wreck.

As for my attire, I chose black with a hint of red on my crown. I found some fitted black pants and a button-down black dress shirt with short sleeves. It was fall, so my suede calf-high boots could now come out of hiding. To cover the front of my hair line I wore a thick, fire-red hair band that pulled my shoulder-length hair behind my ears. I also wore small diamonds in my ears. Yes, they are a girl's best friend, and I felt confident they would sparkle in the stage lights.

After taking several deep breaths it was time to walk through the door. I reached for the large handle with my right hand and pulled the door open. It was heavy and I wasn't used to feeling so weak. When I was heavier I could pull a boat, but now I couldn't even open the door wide enough with one hand to let me inside. It was time to perform and I had to make sure I was on point.

I entered the old church from the back. It had been turned into a black box theatre years ago. The top of the ramped audience was near the doors and when I walked in I could either go right or left to make my way to the holding area for the auditions. Why was this decision so difficult?

The ramped audience obstructed my view and I couldn't see where the director sat or how many people were in the room. I wanted to make a quick, but grand, entrance; I chose the left.

As I quickly walked in I worked to elongate my neck. I swore the girl that I passed to find a seat noticed my chiseled jaw bone. How could anyone miss it? I stretched my legs as long as my black pants would allow, stepping up the risers and making my way to a seat.

I was late and the auditions had begun. It was freezing. I can't perform in cold weather. I can't do anything in cold weather, not even sleep. Since my weight loss, cold weather had become my enemy. And cold to me is not the same as cold to most people. My body cannot withstand temperatures below 55 degrees without severely shaking. This symptom was a side effect of my weight loss. I began to breathe even deeper, pulling my legs and arms as close to me as possible. I had to somehow stay warm so I could succeed. There was only one lead female part and I was determined to get it.

More than 20 women were sitting in the room with me waiting for their chance to read for the role of "Rose Maxson" in August Wilson's *Fences*. Rose is the wife of the leading male character. During the play she and her husband kiss, reference having sex, and she is portrayed as being sexually desirable.

I sat and watched the other women audition for the part in front of Professor Ruffin, who was helming this show. They were all ages and sizes. From old to young adult, short to tall, and small to fat, each woman read the best way she knew how. By the time my name was called, I was furiously shaking. I had failed to keep the cold away and it was starting to affect my brain. I just needed to get somewhere warm, and quick. I wanted to call my winter-induced shaking to Professor Ruffin's attention but I knew he would chalk it up to bad nerves.

As I got up I extended my legs and proceeded to walk to the stage. The lights were on. Stage lights are usually hot, so this was actually the better spot in the room. At this point in the audition I had to read with an older man from the community who was later cast as the male lead in *Fences*. This actor's name is Willie Cogshell.

★★★

Sharrell: Do you think Rose works better as a bigger or smaller woman?
Willie: Smaller.

Sharrell: Why?

Willie: I didn't see her as that big mama; that grandmotherly looking. I didn't see Rose as that because in her role it came out that she did everything she could. Troy [Rose's husband] had no reason to leave and go outside of the marriage. If he had this big woman, [infidelity] would've made more sense. Even the women in the audience would probably say I don't blame him.

Sharrell: For cheating on Rose if she were a big lady?

Willie: For cheating on the big lady.

Sharrell: But because I am small you think it made that scene when I discovered that you were cheating on me more effective?

Willie: Right. It was like there she is. She looks great. Why would he step out on her? That type of thing. Compared to seeing this woman rolling around the stage, you know. I mean that's just the way it is.

★★★

Willie hurt my feelings during that interview. As much as I wanted to stay neutral I couldn't help but think about how awful it is to be a big woman. So one's largeness gives her partner the right to cheat on her? I was so glad that I was smaller.

I told Willie that I had actually gained three more pounds since we last saw each other. He said he didn't notice.

I point out my weight gain a lot now. I am always wondering what the cutoff weight is for men. What is the weight at which I stop receiving the privileges of a slender woman? I laughed at Willie's fat jokes, and my feelings associated with the laughter were the same feelings I experienced as a child when I would laugh with my peers who were scoffing at my fatness. The laughter was undergirded with despair and shame.

★★★

Willie is about 6'3", big-bellied, and has a laugh that reminds you of an old man from Alabama. He seemed to swallow me on stage during the auditions. I felt so small next to him. I'm not used to feeling small next to anyone, but he made me shrink. The only way I could appear as big as him on stage was to use my booming voice. I can get pretty loud. That's one thing that didn't disappear with my pounds: my voice. I began to project and he and I had great chemistry. He reached over to touch me on my arm and I touched him back.

Professor Ruffin began to laugh at our line delivery, which was a good sign. Now I was shaking because I was cold *and* nervous. I took deep breaths to stop the shaking but it wasn't working. So I just gave in to the cold and made peace with my body trembling on stage from head to toe. "I'm cold!" I finally bellowed. No one seemed to care.

Towards the end of the audition, Professor Ruffin dismissed several women and asked me to stay. I read again with Willie and started to realize that I might actually get the role. As I walked across the stage in my slender body I was very aware of what my stomach was doing and how my face was angled. I purposely hadn't eaten a lot before auditions so I could appear smaller.

When we were getting ready to leave Willie was not paying me any attention. I couldn't understand how he couldn't notice me or flirt with me. By this time, I had started to realize that most men viewed me as pretty, but I would often retreat to low self-esteem if the man didn't acknowledge me with a flirtatious gesture. Maybe he didn't flirt because he and I were 20 years apart or maybe he just wasn't focused on me at the time.

I needed him to notice me. I couldn't bear any more public rejections. I'd already been rejected by so many men in my life.

As I picked up my belongings to leave the auditions, I bid Professor Ruffin farewell and walked into the crisp, cool night. I had again succeeded at keeping my secret to myself. The slender person the director just experienced was really not me. I got in my car and headed home, immediately calling my mother to let her know that I'd had a pretty good audition. I reminded her that casting is always unpredictable and that she shouldn't get her hopes up about the role.

Once I reached my house, I took off my clothes, warmed up a meal, and reflected on the day. I felt like a secret service agent, as I always do. I am free in the confines of my home, at least sometimes. I don't have to perform weight loss in my house.

After two days, I got an e-mail with the cast list. I had received the part of "Rose Maxson." A read through was scheduled for the Tuesday after Thanksgiving break. Shucks! I have to make sure and not eat a bunch over Thanksgiving! I thought. For a moment I was very happy, but then I started to think about all of the sexual touching and banter in the play and I cringed. I couldn't kiss worth nothing; hadn't had much practice. How was I going to pull this off again? I couldn't let my secret out of the bag and I couldn't let anyone know that I was afraid of being touched or loved, even if it was make believe.

THE IDEAL SIZE

Sharrell:	What is your ideal Rose?
Professor Ruffin/Director:	You.
Sharrell:	(*laughing*) No, I'm serious.
Professor Ruffin/Director:	Your size is ideal. You know I still feel as though, I don't feel like I have to conform to this idea that if you're a mama and you're a hard-working wife and all that, that you can't be thin or fair-skinned or whatever, but I do believe that you know there is a certain area where you need to fall into that perspective because this is what the audience has seen and the audience will buy and so forth and so on…and so for Rose I think that there is a middle ground where she can't be too skinny, she can't be too big, OK, because of our preconceived [notions]. Rose is a woman, according to her speech, who has desires. She is a sexual being who has desires and an important part of the relationship between Rose and Troy is that Troy sees her as a sexual being.

BITCHES ARE BEAUTIFUL

I was hanging out at a friend of a friend's house. Wearing a big curly wig and a red baby doll dress with a black belt cinched around my waist, I sat quietly at the kitchen bar.

"Timothy, this is my friend Sharrell, yep." My best friend, Rahbi, was introducing me to several of his homies at the house party.

I offered a mini smile. "Hi."

Over the next 30 minutes or so, I had a chance to take in the mustard-colored walls covered in cheap paintings, and a large candelabra.

"Sharrell, you ready to go?" The night was ending much sooner than I thought. "We should go," Rahbi said.

As I settled into the car, Rahbi blurted out, "He called you a bitch."

Baffled. "Who?"

"Timothy." Rahbi kept his eyes on the road.

"A bitch, why? What did I do?"

"I don't know. He just said you seemed like a bitch."

"Me? A bitch?" The logic was clearly missing. All I did was sit at the kitchen bar and sip on a drink.

Throwing his hands up in the air. "Maybe it's because you weren't talking to anybody."

Perplexed. "Yeah, but I never talk to anybody, and no one ever cares."

"I don't know Sharrell. You just have to be nice now."

"Really?" Looking at Rahbi's beard that was growing back in and thinking hard.

"Yeah, you know, people see you. You're pretty and you're not paying anyone any attention. They're going to think you're stuck up. Tyra Banks talks about this too. She says she has to be really nice."

An eerie happiness set in as I realized I was having the "you have to be nice because you're pretty" moment. Laughing, "Rahbi, oh my God, I'm suddenly a bitch just because. This is great!"

"Yeeeeeppp." We celebrated all the way home.

UNSPOKEN EXPECTATIONS

The first thing I did to prepare for *Fences* was to place myself on a low-calorie diet. I pulled out my journal and drafted a "1500-calories-or-less" diet plan.

Diet Plan

8 a.m. – 290 calories (diet shake and banana)

11 a.m. – 400 calories (peanut butter/jelly sandwich and diet shake)

2 p.m. – 200 calories (diet shake and carrots)

5 p.m. – 320 calories (TV dinner—healthy version)

8 p.m. – 290 calories (diet shake and yogurt)

This diet was mandatory because there is an unspoken expectation that the actress will maintain her body weight throughout the rehearsal process and the run of the show.

★★★

As I was in my bed concocting an exercise routine to complement my diet plan the phone rang. "Hello." I spoke softly because I didn't recognize the number.

"Hey gal." Definitely an old man.

I laughed a little. "Who is this?"

"You know who this is. Quit playing. It's Willie."

My voice relaxed. "Hey Willie. How … are … you?" I dragged the question out to reveal a tone of deep curiosity as to why he was calling.

"Awe girl quit acting like you don't wanna talk to me."

I laughed. "That is not how I sound."

"Anyway, I got your number from the cast list. I tried to e-mail you but the e-mail wouldn't go through." He was lying and I knew it. I figured he just didn't know how to use e-mail. "Yeah, so we need to work on our onstage romantic chemistry."

"Really? You think so?"

I wasn't sexually attracted to Willie, not that I had to be, but the attraction would've helped. And I wasn't excited to work on our romantic scenes because of my hang-ups with my weight and not feeling cute. But Willie was right. "OK, Willie. Let's work on it sometime next week."

"Awe girl, what's wrong? You don't wanna kiss an old man?"

Why did he have to remind me that he was damn near a senior citizen. I laughed some more. "You're funny. But yeah, let's work on the kissing and stuff next week."

Willie proceeded to tell me that he was in a show once in which the guy and girl actors whose characters were in love decided to go on outings together. I knew where this conversation was going and a part of me was flattered but the other part was trying to figure out how to say no to him. The sensual connection was necessary, but I figured we could do that type of chemistry building work in rehearsal.

Figure 3.1: Sharrell, the "fly" years.

FRACTURED

Talk "Fat" Session

I broke. Down. Sideways. Across. Slipped. Lost myself. My body changed fast. Too fast. I broke. My mind couldn't keep up. Or maybe my mind broke long before and my body couldn't keep up. So she stretched out. And when she snapped back, seemed like everybody wanted to watch. I felt like a new cast member in "Beverly Hills 90210." Now I know it shoulda' been "A Different World," but no, it was definitely "Beverly Hills." Or was it Beverly Hills in my body, and a different world in my mind? Either way, I had safely transitioned from one location to another, from one conscience to another, but it was the *almost* fight that terrified me. Not because I was going to fight a dude, but because I couldn't calm Fat Sharrell down. Yes, she was there. And she was in control at that moment, and I couldn't save me from myself. Before that altercation, I assumed I was whole. Up until that point I hadn't realized I'd been mediating different voices in my mind; distinct voices that either kept me hungry or kept me fed.

Soon after I lost weight, away in Missouri in grad school, clear distinctions between selves emerged. Fine-tuned voices that kept me in the gym or kept me buying 12-pack grab bags of Cheetos took hold of my psyche. And one day, when I was analyzing data for my autoethnography, these identities began to converse with one another. This is when I realized that as a transweight person, parts of me were displaced or even (re)membered during and after my transition. It felt like I hadn't packed enough for the journey and at other times it felt like I had packed too much. My transweight status had left me psychologically altered or fractured. I broke. My mind split into three identities; Fat Sharrell, Skinny Sharrell, and Liminal Sharrell (the mediator).

While analyzing her data on the lived experiences of Black women in the context of their lover identities, socio–cultural literacist Jeanine Staples identified the emergence of fractured identities. In conversation with the research of Elizabeth de Freitas and Jillian Paton,[1] Staples' defined fractured identities as

> iteration[s] of one's collective identity … performed as aspects of Self because they voice one particular sensibility in fairly unilateral ways; they articulate an individual's dominant inclinations through language and its effects … They simply express and pursue mani-festation. They are only focused on giving voice to the stories and inherent sensibility of the person they belong to, given the aspect of Self they represent.[2]

While engaging with the narratives of fractured selves in Staples' research, I came to recognize my distinct identities as fragments of myself. Fat Sharrell and Skinny Sharrell are a part of my full being, while occupying deep spaces of resistance towards one another. But unlike Staples' theory that these identities only give voice as manifestation of the aspect of the self they represent—in my own experience, and subsequent work on myself that I did, and that I am in the process of doing—I find that my fractured identities are both particular and plural. And while they speak from a manifestation of my own embodied self, they are engaged in a dialogue establishing the wholeness of the woman that I am striving to be. And while Liminal Sharrell mediates, she also modulates not just the voices, as in cases of split personalities—she varies, interprets, and interpolates meaning between—not just Fat or Skinny Sharrell, but the always present voices of Skinny Sharrell within Fat Sharrell and Fat Sharrell within Skinny Sharrell. Hence these are not distinct mani-festations but the yearning and fears of the perennially present Sharrell that is always and already negotiating her processes of being and becoming.

I discovered that Fat Sharrell is "the old me," the fat me; my fat psyche. She is a leader, a fighter, and a suppressed sex siren. She is my mama's "teddy bear" who eats at the table hunched over, hoarding her plate so her big ass brother can't get any of her food. She is stingy and mean. She has learned to hate herself because she sees herself through the eyes of men.

Skinny Sharrell adorns the word "skinny" though she is really slender. Understand, no matter how much weight the body gains back, Skinny Sharrell is skinny. She knows this, and she loves this. She can cross her legs, laugh freely, and invoke video vixen at any second. She's more than a lil fast too. Skinny Sharrell is on edge, and freer in bed, but her lust is contradictory. She likes to exercise. She is smart, but she is not a leader. She has learned to love herself because she sees herself through the eyes of men.

The mediator is the (I) identity, which I have termed Liminal Sharrell. Liminal Sharrell is the psyche that straddles Fat Sharrell and Skinny Sharrell. Liminal Sharrell consciously theorizes from the hyphen (-). She has dual knowledge of different embodied experiences. She sees herself through the eyes of her mother and father. Liminal Sharrell wants everybody to get along, to be friends, but Fat and Skinny are always at odds. Always. So the day that they appeared on the page, Liminal Sharrell let them speak.

The fractured identities began to dialogue once they encountered written diaries and video diaries that were kept throughout the rapid weight loss diet. I didn't stop them. I needed to hear what they had to say. Hence, in the proceeding pages, coupled with several diary entries, is commentary from my slender psyche (Skinny Sharrell), my fat psyche (Fat Sharrell), and the psyche that straddles fat and skinny (Liminal Sharrell). This psychological trifecta fussed with each other, challenged one another, and longed to stay separate, even as they worked together to protect me.

Reader's Reflection #2

Would you be, or have you been accepting of a fat actress cast in a sexually desirable leading lady role? Why or why not?

NOTES

1 Elizabeth de Freitas and Jillian Paton, "(De)facing the Self: Poststructural Disruptions of the Autoethnographic Text," *Qualitative Inquiry* 15, no. 3 (2009): 483–498.

2 Jeanine M. Staples, *The Revelations of Asher: Toward Supreme Love in Self* (New York: Peter Lang Publishing, 2016), 21.

CHAPTER 4

MAINTENANCE

December 1, 2010
176 pounds

By the opening of *Fences*, I am trying to lose a total of 100 pounds. I'm only 12 pounds away from reaching my goal.

Liminal Sharrell: I'm scared. I want to reach a place of acceptance.

Fat Sharrell: I'm afraid I'll come back to myself very soon, but I will welcome her skinniness with open arms. I think what she did was amazing. But she hides me, every bit of my beauty. I believe I made Sharrell who she is today, and she at least owes me a "thank you." As I disappeared, she did everything to permanently keep me out. Starving herself, exercising rigorously, and telling people how much she hated me, but I loved her and I still do. I love you Sharrell.

Skinny Sharrell: Sharrell needs to stop eating so I can fit comfortably in my size 8s and 10s. Get it together girl! You can do this! Hold on, hold on tight. I bring you happiness and men. You know you love men. If you can just lose a few more pounds, you will do the unthinkable. Just stop eating. No matter what, all women want to be thin. Don't let the media and counselors and Fat Studies folk tell you that it's okay to be fat because it's not. I know you want the world to embrace your fatness, but the world won't do that. We have to keep conforming. You must stay skinny.

December 7, 2010
176 pounds

Well, today took a turn for the worse. I went to get measurements for my costume and discovered that my belly had grown from a size 31 to a size 34. I felt really sad. I wasn't really dreading the process until she actually put the measuring tape on my body. Then I realized she was going to produce numbers. Ugh! I haven't exercised in approximately 11 days and the way this weather is going, I don't see me exercising a lot this season.

Liminal Sharrell:	I haven't exercised for the past 2 weeks. I have to do better.
Fat Sharrell:	Looks like I'm on my way back.
Skinny Sharrell:	They say that when people find me, they lose me. But not Sharrell. She's past the two-year mark, and I'm still with her, but I am starting to disappear a little bit. Sharrell, what's going on?
Liminal Sharrell:	I'm trying!
Skinny Sharrell:	Try harder.
Fat Sharrell:	Do you really hate me that much?
Liminal Sharrell:	(silence).

★★★

The moon is crawling in my stomach. Hunger pangs make me weak. The day usually starts off good. By 2 p.m. I've only consumed 600 calories, but when the sun sets, the hunger monster comes out to play. I "eat walk" every night.

The kitchen cabinets get opened about 20 times between 5 p.m. and 10 p.m. I consume bags of cheese potato chips. Then I pop popcorn and tell myself that I should just eat wholesome food. So I microwave a healthy TV dinner, and in that five minutes of waiting, I scarf down two yogurt cups with granola.

After finishing the small meal, I remember the chocolate bar that is stashed in my bedroom. While I rest my feet on the glass coffee table the chocolate melts in my mouth.

My eyes run across the weight loss books housed on the living room shelves. I think about the things I should be eating for my blood type. I think about how I don't really care for meat. Then I think harder about what I'm going to eat the next day. I promise myself the diet will begin tomorrow. I make the "diet" promise to myself nearly every night.

★★★

Video Diary
176 pounds

I'm crying because I feel horrible. I think I'm going to have to make losing weight like a religion. I feel that no one understands my struggle. I can't gain this weight back, and it scares me. It's so hard. It's so hard, really hard. There is so much pressure, and I want to eat. I feel like I can't be normal. I can't be normal. I keep asking myself what do I want more than food? I like looking pretty as a smaller person. My brain is tired, and I'm constantly thinking. My goal for *Fences* was to lose the weight, and I feel like I can't. I'm five pounds bigger than last year. Maybe I should build a fence around myself.

Liminal Sharrell: Still trying to be normal.

Fat Sharrell: I'm definitely abnormal.

Skinny Sharrell: I'm not sure that I'm normal. I feel normal, but then I also feel average. I look around and notice that other people are just like me. I'm right at the threshold of plus-size clothes. I need to get even smaller to be normal in my book.

December 9, 2010
176 pounds

You know, I've been really putting myself last in my food decision choices. I have been doing what everybody but me wants to do. I have subjected myself to eating at restaurants, which is an automatic failure for me. Now, I know it doesn't have to be, but I don't even like eating out that much, so when I go out to eat, I like to get what I want. I need rules. Rules that I abide by; that I won't change. Rules such as eat out only twice a month. I need my stamina back; my belief in myself that I can really do this. No matter what, I promised myself that I would never stop making rules or exercise schedules. Why? Because I never stopped going on diets all those years. I believed somewhere deep down inside that I could one day lose a large amount of weight and I did.

Liminal Sharrell:

1 Create a new fitness plan and stick to it
2 No eating after 9 p.m.
3 Eat more vegetables
4 Find Sharrell
5 Study my lines for the show

Fat Sharrell:

1 Find Sharrell
2 Eat anytime I get hungry
3 Enjoy the sweets in life
4 Hang around other fat people

Skinny Sharrell:

1 Lose 20 pounds
2 Do not buy larger clothes no matter what
3 Exercise four to five times a week
4 Take lots of pictures

December 20, 2010
178.5 pounds

Long-Term Goals:

1 Lose 15.5 pounds
2 Eat more veggies
3 Decrease sugar intake
4 Decrease sodium intake

Short-Term Goals to Start Reaching Long-Term Goals:

1 Walk at least 30 min./4 days a week
2 Eat one vegetable a day
3
4

Skinny Sharrell:	Is there something to be said about the blank goal lines above? Maybe this is why you can't seem to reach your ultimate goal because you can't focus long enough to write four goals.
Liminal Sharrell:	Why does it have to be four goals?
Skinny Sharrell:	You're the one who wrote the numbers.
Liminal Sharrell:	No, you wrote them. So why didn't you finish?
Skinny Sharrell:	Because I'm incomplete.
Fat Sharrell:	Have me back?
Liminal Sharrell:	No

SECRETS ARE FOR THE SEXY

The red ladybug panties hugged my small, still-square ass as I posed for a back shot selfie in my hallway mirror. I had 20 more panties in the striped pink bag with hot pink ribbons as handles. Earlier that day I had trailed a few steps behind Mia as she entered Victoria's Secret, a popular lingerie shop whose underwear sizes go up to XL.

The panties laid out at the front of the store had colorful slogans slapped on the butt area such as "cute," "sexy," and "smart." Ice cream cones, metallic flowers, and stars were found on other panties.

I leaned down to the bottom drawer, looking for the XL. "What you doing?" Mia asked.

"Looking for my size."

"All the way down there?" Mia leaned on one of her bowed legs as she rummaged through medium sized underwear.

"What size do you think I wear?"

"A medium or a large," she said frankly while trying not to stare at my crotch and hips.

My face turned as I was working to imagine my butt in the very small looking medium and large sized underwear. But I had to trust Mia. Surely she knew because she was about a size smaller than me.

I hesitantly picked out 21 pairs of size medium panties and purchased them. Here was an opportunity to adorn my body with colorful hues; an opportunity that I was robbed of as a fat child.

Two months later, I had amassed over 65 Victoria's Secret panties, opened a credit card in the store, and maxed it out. I was in underwear heaven. No more department store undies for me.

Shopping in the very pink store made me feel so girly, so feminine, and a member of an elite group of women.

WHEN YOU KNOW IT'S REAL

My size 24 and size 26 jeans were nice. I owned lovely sequin and lace dresses from Lane Bryant, Ashley Stewart, Fashion Bug, and the plus size department in Macy's.

I also had a special relationship with blue jeans. I probably owned 25 pairs. My large clothes were full of painful memories and drenched in fruity perfume. These items now rested in a complete mess in black garbage bags in my mama's basement. I was holding on tight to them because I knew how most weight loss stories ended; most gained the weight back, and then some. But after two years, I felt it was time to let go of a portion of my past.

Instead of taking the five full black trash bags to the Goodwill, I bagged them up and drove to a nearby clothing bin. This act of release had to be quick if I were to accomplish "letting go." As I re-examined the contents in one bag, I smiled and laughed at the many memories that surfaced: horrible clubbing experiences, rejection, and suicide watch parties had with friends.

Was I really going to do this? Once I put my fat clothes in the bin there was no sure way to get them back. Am I really going to stay small?

It began to rain: a baptism into my slender life, maybe.

I lifted the first heavy bag and ran towards the dumpster, silently praying, "Please let these clothes be a blessing to a big girl somewhere." I opened the bin and pushed the bag down the chute. Anger, frustration, and happiness consumed me all at once. A sigh of relief. My big girl past was leaving me.

I hurried to the car so that I didn't have time to change my mind, hoisted the second bag onto my shoulder, ran to the dumpster, and shoved it into the bin. More silent prayers were said: "Let her love the clothes. Let her feel the struggle and pain that they covered. Let her love the clothes as she hopefully loves herself."

After a few more trips to the bin, there was nothing left to carry. I looked back at the dumpster while the rain cascaded down my brown face, mixing with the tears that were there first.

The back of my car was empty. Like the fat on my body, I wanted my beautiful big girl clothes to disappear forever.

GOING UP

December 26, 2010
180.8 pounds

Well, the digital home scale just weighed me in at 180.8. Even when I've eaten a lot, the scale will weigh me in between 176 and 177, so I've done some serious damage. I keep thinking about *Fences,* and I don't feel as much pressure to remain thin because it's not that type of character. I want to be cute, but she doesn't have to be. She gets cheated on. I want to lose this weight for myself though because I know I will feel much better on that stage as a smaller person. Yesterday was awful. I ate Chinese food, a Caesar salad, pizza, a TV dinner, potato chips, brownies, and broccoli. Oh, I had some cheesecake too.

Fat Sharrell:	Before I disappeared, cheesecake was my favorite dessert. I would crave it all the time and eat it whenever I could. I loved plain cheesecake and marble cheesecake. The cream melting in my mouth and the hint of cheese made me feel like I was floating away.
Skinny Sharrell:	When I appeared, I thought I would love cheesecake too. I have no desire to eat it. It doesn't make me happy. I wish I liked it, but I don't. I like Kettle Baked Chips: Cheddar & Sour Cream, to be exact.

★★★

January 7, 2011
180 pounds

I now weigh 180 pounds. So very sad. Anyhow, I remembered that when I have heavy breakfasts, they hold me for a very long time. So I created a new meal plan that allows me to have options. I used my knowledge of my eating habits from the past 2 years and created a plan that I believe works for me. If I can curtail the hunger, then I can curtail the weight gain and start dropping. So now, I am really trying to lose 20 pounds. Seems like that number keeps rising. I also read that when you don't get enough sleep, your body overproduces the hormone that signals hunger and under produces the hormone that signals fullness.

Meal Plan

8 a.m.	10 a.m.	12 p.m.	2 p.m.	4 p.m.	6 p.m.	8 p.m.
Shake, Oatmeal/ toast, or Egg beaters and fake sausage 170 calories	Fruit 100 cal	Salad, Clif Bar, or Lunchable 250 calories	Shake 170 cal	Shake, Yogurt, or Fruit 170 calories	Protein, veggies 400 cal	Fruit, Yogurt, or Treat 170 calories

Fat Sharrell: I remember I used to wish I weighed 200 pounds. I knew I'd be fine and life would be grand. I remember when the weight loss doctor told me that I'd probably reach 185 pounds. I totally didn't believe her. I thought she was doing a bit of wishful thinking. I remember not being loved. I remember it all. I remember the hunger and the crying spells and the nights I held you.

Liminal Sharrell: I read so much about the war on obesity. I buy books frequently that include weight loss stories and pictures. I get e-mails from weight loss companies with tips to shape up for the summer and survive the holiday food season. I learn something new about the body every day. God knew what She was doing when she made me. I operate perfectly.

Skinny Sharrell: It's almost 11 p.m. I should go to bed.

ALMOST SHOWTIME

January 15, 2011
177.7 pounds

Hey! The holidays are over and rehearsals for *Fences* are about to start back up. I must remain weight conscious. And I'm starting to believe that reintegration into society is nearly impossible because I always have to eat, thus I'm always thinking about what I'm putting in my mouth.

Fat Sharrell: I always thought about what I put into my mouth.

Skinny Sharrell: I'm always thinking about what I'm putting into my mouth.

Liminal Sharrell: I'm always thinking that I wish I didn't have to think about what to put in my mouth.

★★★

102

Ways That Liminal Sharrell Performs Slenderness:

1   I always look at the medium sized clothing first when shopping.
2   I simply act as if I'm not hungry.
3   Giggle a lot around men.
4   When I know someone is looking my way I give a nice profile and make sure my jaw bone is prominent.

★★★

January 18, 2011
177 pounds

I'm exhausted. Rehearsal today was cool. I felt sexy cuz I've been slightly starving myself for three days now. Being cute in rehearsal is important to me. It's several dudes in this show, and I want all of them to like me. I want to feel small around them too. Like a dainty princess trying to find her way.

Liminal Sharrell:	I get ravenously hungry. I have thoughts of fasting but I have usually failed by 10 a.m. I've actually had a voracious appetite these last few days. I keep eating as long as I'm hungry.
Fat Sharrell:	I could never starve myself.
Skinny Sharrell:	I can starve myself. I do it all the time, just not lately. I feel a starvation period coming on though. I need to starve myself to stay around. I must stay around.
Liminal Sharrell:	I keep Skinny Sharrell from starving me. I don't know if I'm afraid of success or not. I do want to lose a total of 100 pounds, but for some reason I don't equate food with fatness. I think I need to.
Fat Sharrell:	Food is always equated with me. I would eat fast food two to three times a day and still eat cooked food at home. I still declare that I am not an emotional eater. I eat because the food tastes good.
Liminal Sharrell:	I eat because the food tastes good.
Skinny Sharrell:	I eat because the food helps me to survive.

CHIVALRY IS ALIVE AND WELL

It was about 20 degrees outside. I opened the theatre door and the frost began to set on my face.

"Sharrell, do you mind if I walk you to your car?"

I froze just like the weather. "Sure, that's fine."

Brendan was a brown-skinned younger actor in *Fences*. He was talented but not really my type. I tend to like them older and cuter. As we briskly walked through the weather, my mind was racing. I thought he had a girlfriend, and I know he preaches the Gospel. Why does he want to walk with me? Is this what chivalry feels like? Oh, no, what if he asks for my phone number? What do I do?

"It's a nice evening, don't you think?" He sniffled, and then inhaled the cold air and blew it out, showing his slanted, crowded bottom teeth.

"Yeah, it's pretty cool," I responded, feeling really strange. I wanted to scream at him and tell him to go away because I didn't know what was expected of me after he walked me to my car.

As we approached the car, I unlocked the door, and he opened it for me. "Thank you." I sounded confused while I made it a point not to look at him.

"You're welcome. Good night." He turned to leave.

He's a cheater, I thought. All these church boys are cheaters. I can't believe him! Walking me to my car. "Thanks Brendan." A partial smile appeared on my face as I watched him like a hawk. I thought about that evening for about a week. The night was simply bizarre to me.

Nothing ever came of it.

I wanted to be flattered but didn't quite make it to that state of mind because I was always waiting for the "catch."

★★★

Fat Sharrell:	Dudes never walked me to my car. Never!
Liminal Sharrell:	Immediately I think he must want me. He's surely hitting on me. But I have to tell him about my past if we are to go any further. If they don't know my past, then I feel like they don't know me.
Skinny Sharrell:	You don't have to tell them anything.
Fat Sharrell:	Walks to cars are the kind of thing I can only dream of. I can't even fathom someone randomly talking to me. I swear I don't have low self-esteem. I can always tell that no one wants to get to know me. I mean I've had relationships, but I fell into most of them. None of them started with attraction.

Dressing the Body

January 27, 2011
177 pounds

So I went to my *Fences* costume fitting. Ugh! Hell! I was a little scared and I announced to Professor Ruffin and the costumer that I'd probably gained five pounds since my measurements were taken and that I was working diligently to lose weight before the show opened. We all laughed, but I was hurting somewhere deep down inside. I couldn't let them see that though. I was so relieved to see how big the dresses were, and how they draped over my body.

The first dress was colorful paisley with an apron and some brown shoes. I liked the movement that it enabled and my fat arms were fully covered. Because Professor Ruffin had already worked with me, he knew how badly I felt about my arms and made sure to cover them up. My arms were wonderfully hidden so I felt like some real acting could take place. As the seamstress nipped and tucked my costumes, I thought about how I really wanted to be much smaller. My glance went from the mirror to my director back to the mirror and to my inner thoughts of skinniness. Why must losing weight be this difficult? Why?

Liminal Sharrell:	I think about my size every time I look in the mirror. I want so badly to be smaller.
Skinny Sharrell:	My arms irk me. They don't fit. They are the one indication that I'm not normal. That something used to be wrong with me. The fat on my arms is like smudges on a new car. I want it gone. I am trying to put the thought in Sharrell's mind to consider having the skin on her arms removed, but she won't hear it.
Liminal Sharrell:	I won't hear it. I'm scared of surgery.
Skinny Sharrell:	I think she'll do it though. Once she reaches her goal weight.
Fat Sharrell:	Cutting the skin off would mean that I would never be welcomed back.
Liminal Sharrell:	I can't cut the skin off. It's a part of me. It reminds me of someone lost. Someone who I wish I could talk to.
Fat Sharrell:	I will love you even harder when I come back. It will be just me and you. Just like old times.

STABILITY?

January 28, 2011
178 pounds

Willie is getting more comfortable with touching me and I admit it feels really good when he does. I've never felt this small in my life. He likes to approach me from the back and put his whole arm around me. We were blocking a scene in which I congratulate him on a job promotion and the director told me to run downstage and give Willie a hug. When I did this, he hugged me back and easily lifted me waaaaay off my feet and twirled me around. I felt so light, so free, so happy. A man was actually lifting me up and enjoying doing it. He felt so good and I was a little taken aback so I had to control my reaction. I wasn't sure if he was making that routine in the show but I sure as hell hope so. I have to admit that I want to be twirled around for all to see.

Liminal Sharrell: I felt like a real girl. I felt like I was in a movie and I was believably the leading lady whom anybody could fall in love with.

Fat Sharrell: I've never been picked up in my life.

★★★

February 4, 2011
178 pounds

Yesterday I wore a nice wig to rehearsal with some fitted clothes. The men in the cast thought I was cute. It made me feel good even though I could tell from the way the clothes fit that I had put on a little extra weight. I can see it in my pictures too. I just look plumper. Bigger. Fatter. Not pleased with myself. Now when I put on clothes I'm wondering if I can wear them. That's not good but it's the truth. I am busting out of my pants. My belly is bigger and my thighs are bigger. And when you're smaller every little bit counts. A centimeter means a lot to a big toe.

Skinny Sharrell: I will not force myself to wear a larger size. I will fit in the clothes that you bought me.

Fat Sharrell: You threw all my clothes away. You just left me with big skirts because you think you can make them look like full body dresses. That means that you are rid of me for good. Is this true? Why did you throw my outfits away?

Liminal Sharrell:	I have to let go at some point. I can't hoard all of that stuff. Once I didn't immediately welcome you back into my life, I decided that I had to make a serious choice. By keeping those big clothes, I was saying that I was some-day going to be very big again. I stepped out on faith and threw my past away.
Fat Sharrell:	Not all of it though.
Liminal Sharrell:	You're right.
Skinny Sharrell:	What?
Fat Sharrell:	You still have those clothes that you wore the day you began to starve yourself.
Liminal Sharrell:	I do.
Fat Sharrell:	Why did you keep them?
Liminal Sharrell:	Because they mean a lot to me. They mean more to me than any other piece of clothing I've purchased since I became smaller. That day I was being myself. My true self. Hair, clothes, arms and all. I showed it all to the world, and I think it was the first day I began to love myself. I smiled for the camera and I think I was happy. I didn't have that faraway look in my eye. I had a look of hope, of determination, of freedom.
Fat Sharrell:	Do you miss me?
Liminal Sharrell:	Sometimes.
Skinny Sharrell:	I never think about you, fatty.
Fat Sharrell:	I never think about you either.

★★★

February 17, 2011
180 pounds

Yesterday was my first day not being sexy during rehearsal. I felt hor-rible. I had on sweat pants with a yellow long-sleeved shirt with a knit hat and none of it matched at all and I felt grimy. I'm wondering what I am not saying. So if one were to ask me that, I would say I'm not saying how much pressure I feel to perform well in this role. I'm not saying how I've been thinking about my stretch marks a lot lately and how I feel when men finally see me with my clothes off. I fear they immediately know that something about my body is different; that my skin is abnormally stretched, though it doesn't hang. No one has said anything yet, but I wonder. Maybe the men that I've had sex with since I've lost weight need to be the ones that I interview. In my conversations with Willie I am very pompous about my looks and I even said to him last night, "Oh, you haven't seen my legs yet!" Does this show low self-esteem? What do pretty girls talk about with boys? I thought yesterday about how much my mom is going to enjoy seeing me onstage as a smaller woman again. I am not ashamed of how I look on stage.

Liminal Sharrell:	I'm not saying how disappointed I am in myself for not reaching my ultimate goal. I'm not saying how lost I feel right now in this liminal space. I'm not saying how I really do want to apologize to Fat Sharrell for not loving her like I should have.
Skinny Sharrell:	I'm not saying how hungry I am.
Fat Sharrell:	I'm not saying how I know if Sharrell does come back to me that she would more than likely get rid of me again. I'm not saying how I don't like myself either. I'm not saying how much I want men to like me. I'm not saying how much it hurts to live in a world that hates you.

JUDGMENT-FREE EATING

"Anybody want anything from McDonald's?" Mikki asked. She was playing the role of the little girl in *Fences*. Mikki, with her very small 5'1" frame canvassed the cast with her eyes while we were all in the wings taking a break and chatting. One cast member reached in his wallet and gave her a bill, placing his order.

The yellow-ish potato fries danced in my mind. I had sworn off fries successfully for over two years. I was fighting with myself, and had been eating more unhealthy foods lately. Mikki turned to leave.

"Mikki!" I was surprised that I called her name.

I received no evil stares from anyone. No one suggested that I skip McDonald's or eat a salad. No one suggested that I share with them. Good. I was in the clear to order.

"Mikki! Get me a small fry."

The words hurt my lips, but I meant them. I was an addict going back to the crack house, if only for a morsel. "Just a small fry," I said as Mikki shot me an "are you sure?" glance.

I had told Mikki about my past because she was helping me collect data by taking photos during rehearsal. She was the only one monitoring my eating behavior. If I were fat, the whole damn room would be rolling their eyes at me.

Ignoring her serious gaze, I reached my skinny fingers with visible veins and bones into my purse and handed her a dollar.

When the small order of fries was placed in my hands, the smell took me away to a special place; a spot that I had missed on my tongue and in my belly. This place was made especially for greasy, unhealthy fries and other foods. Unlike my actions in the past, I nibbled on one fry at a time, in the wings, waiting for break to be over. To my delight, I didn't die.

CURTAINS UP ON *FENCES*

February 25, 2011
178.2 pounds

3:17 a.m. I can't sleep. I'm having anxiety. This is why I hate acting. It's not in my blood. It stresses me out, wakes me up in the middle of the night and I go through the show in my mind. I say the wrong lines in my sleep and I wake up as I move through alertness to deliriousness. I touch my back. I feel my rolls. I am disappointed. Extremely disappointed. I've settled for sugar and chocolate every time I felt deprived. I guess this is what they mean when they say you can't have your cake and eat it too. That's a saying for fat folks.

(later that evening)

I fell today in the show. My mama came and I fell. The fall actually complemented the scene, but my shoe flew up in the air. I fell trying to stop my husband and son from fighting. I fell. I've been falling all year. Failing really. I'm panicked and I want everybody to leave me alone so I can figure this thing out. I feel bigger. My stomach is hanging over my pants and the loose skin on my neck is getting wrinkled. I'm getting old too. Maybe I will age quicker now that I have loose skin. I guess I don't want to lose 100 pounds yet. That's what it is. I can't want it because I don't fight for it.

Willie keeps asking about my rehearsal research, but I don't tell him. I don't want to burst the bubble for him. I want to stay the girl that he thinks I am. If he were in the dressing room with me, he would know my secret for sure by now. Every day before the show I have to look at the dangling fat on my arms and the stretch marks that cover my body.

★★★

February 27, 2011
180.5 pounds

Last night was amazing. So many people complimented me on my acting. A professor who specializes in directing said that my performance is one worth remembering and she doesn't remember many. Another professor said that this is the best show he's ever seen at the University of Missouri.

Then this lady told my mom and me that she saw *Fences* on Broadway this year and I performed the role of "Rose" even better than the lady she saw on Broadway. That lady is Viola Davis who recently won the Tony for her portrayal of "Rose" opposite Denzel Washington.

My stomach was still poking out yesterday, and I panicked when I went to put on my costume and it felt tighter. Then I noticed it was faded. The dresser told me it had been washed. It was mainly tighter around my right fat arm. OK, be mindful. I have to be nicer to myself. I'm really proud of myself. Every time I ask myself would I be this happy if I were big? The answer is no. But maybe I do love myself as a human a little more than I did when I was fat. It's hard to untwist 20 years of mental abuse afflicted by myself and other people (mostly men). They denied me. They denied me love and now they want to give it to me. That's hard to accept. I love being small and slender and dainty on that stage. I love it down to the bottom of my soul. The way I move, the way I walk, everything is just easier. Life is just easier.

TOO PRETTY

Sharrell: What did you think about when you saw me in *Fences*?

Mama: Frankly, my honest opinion is you were too pretty to play that part. Weight was not a consideration at all. You were still maintaining and uh, to be a wife who loved her husband and tolerated his drunkenness, umm, you know anyone in that situation from day to day would have a more strained look on her face and have the appearance of someone who has really been through situations with her husband. But you were a pretty woman in that play and that play could have been miscast. But you really jumped into that role and you became Rose. I was very proud of that. One interesting thing happened. The man that I was sitting next to, which happened to be a Caucasian man, after I whispered to someone that you were my daughter, he overheard it and then everybody looked at me and then kind of whispered and this man said "Oh she's so pretty, oh your daughter has a smile. Did you see that smile honey?" He said to his wife. And he said "Oh no doubt, we're gonna see more of her," and he was impressed. Another thing I thought was that you look like my mother. My mother was a beautiful woman. All that I ever heard about her was that she was a beautiful woman and she was a normal-sized woman, I guess about a 14. My mother was always said to have had a beautiful figure and I have a picture of my mother and father's wedding and she's always been a very elegant looking beautiful woman, and I thought about how much Rose looked like my mother who passed away in 2005, and I just had a smile on my face thinking, oh I wish mother could see Sharrell, I wish mother could see Sharrell.

MENDING FENCES

I held the telephone close to my ear. "Willie. So listen. I'm about to tell you something."

"Here you go talking weird again. Shoot. What you got to tell me baby?" Sounding like Barry White on a bad day.

"I used to be bigger."

"Really? How much bigger?"

"Like really big."

"Awe girl get outta here. You pulling my leg. How much bigger?"

"Does it matter?"

"Naw, I guess not, but hell you sayin' that you used to be bigger and I'm just trying to talk to you baby, see where you coming from. I mean it can't be that much bigger."

I spit it out. "I used to be morbidly obese."

"Really? Wow. You lying."

I kept quiet.

"Well congratulations. That's an accomplishment. Man, I wish I could lose some weight. Wow, morbid huh? Bet you won't tell the ole preacher that."

"Don't you say a thing, Willie." I threatened him because I was afraid if Professor Ruffin, the preacher/director found out, then it would make him look at me differently.

"Your secret's safe with me baby."

It pleased me so much that he was still talking to me after my big reveal. I felt so at ease, like I wasn't fooling him anymore.

Liminal Sharrell:	I remember what it's like being fat. I feel myself every day and try to grasp the body I'm living in, but it feels fleeting, like it will be gone any second.
Skinny Sharrell:	It will be gone if you eat that Icebox Cheesecake that's in front of you.
Fat Sharrell:	Do it.
Liminal Sharrell:	I'm going to eat it. I'm going to eat it for me and for you, Skinny Sharrell. Yes for you. I'm tired of you putting me down and telling me to starve myself. I'm tired of counting calories and exercising out of fear. I want to exercise because it makes me feel good. I'm going to eat the cheesecake and then smile afterwards. I'm fighting the guilty feelings that are surfacing right now.
Skinny Sharrell:	Yes, because you know you're gaining weight.
Liminal Sharrell:	So. I can get it off. Leave me alone.
Skinny Sharrell:	Are you sure?
Fat Sharrell:	Eat the cheesecake. Do it for us. It'll be just like old times.
Liminal Sharrell:	No, not old times because I will only eat half.
Fat Sharrell:	Half?
Liminal Sharrell:	Yeah half. Can you believe it? Not because I'm on a diet, but because I've changed. I really have. I may be gaining weight, but I just can't eat as much as I used to.
Fat Sharrell:	Wow.
Skinny Sharrell:	I guess I'm losing this battle.
Liminal Sharrell:	Yes you are losing this battle tonight.
Skinny Sharrell:	Well, you're losing in the long run.

★★★

March 6, 2011
Video Diary
180.5 pounds

Today is the last show. I have been having a blast. I'm in a good mood. I don't feel like talking about my weight. Fuck how much I weigh.

CHAPTER 5

WEIGHTED LOSS

At 183 pounds, I rolled over away from Daryl in the bed to look at my phone. It was 3 a.m. My mama was calling.

Groggy. "Hello."

"Sharrell, come take me to the hospital. I don't feel well."

"Mama. What's wrong? Can't Jamia take you? I know she's laying right there." My mama always yearned for attention from me.

"I don't want to wake her, Sharrell."

"Mama, that makes no sense. Wake her up and tell her to take you to the emergency room and then call and let me know what's going on."

"The vessels in my arm look swollen."

"OK. Ya'll go and then let me know."

"Where are you, gal?" She knew I was with a man.

"I'm at Eric's house, and you know he lives way out." I was really five minutes up the street sleeping with Daryl.

"OK." She let me off the hook.

Later that morning I arrived at the neighborhood hospital to check on my mother. They eventually transferred her to Edinburgh Memorial Hospital because they found an alien substance in her belly that would later be identified as stage 4 cancer.

Fuck cancer.

My mama looked over at me and rolled her eyes from the hospital bed. "I know where you were."

My quirky sister chimed in. "Yeah mama. She was at that man's house." Stretching his name out in a funny manner. "Daaaaaarrrrrryyyyyl." They had driven by his house and seen my car in his driveway before they went to the hospital.

"But mama, Jamia was right next to you." My sister and I couldn't give up our roles as children, even when my mama needed us to.

After a few more minutes of feeling extremely guilty, I asked, "Mama, you want me to finish my dissertation? I can drop out and finish later."

"Naw, Sharrell. I want you to finish."

"But you're in the hospital. Really, it's no big deal. I can finish another time. School isn't going anywhere."

She looked over at me with a serious gaze, "You get your doctorate."

I pulled out my purple laptop and opened it. I always had it on me. While my mama was hooked up to machines and IVs, I sat by her bedside in the hospital working on my dissertation.

"What you writing about now?"

"I'm talking about how all the men like me now, and how I can't deal with it. I'ma put that in my show too."

"I thought you liked the attention?"

I looked over at my mama's almond-shaped eyes and her heart-shaped lips that were now roughly 60 years old. "I do like the attention mama." She was so pretty. "Thank you for giving me your looks." She was flattered like she always was.

"You think I'm pretty? Even now?"

"Yes, mama." I rested my laptop on the cold hospital floor and got up to secure my mama's black and gold scarf in place. She always wanted to look her best. As instructed, I reached in her over-sized purse and handed her her hot red lipstick. I watched her apply it.

"Mama, you can't be putting on lipstick. You 'sposed to be sick."

"This is my face. You might catch you a doctor if you put some on your face. Here." She prompted me to put some lipstick on, but I pushed her hand away. We shared a small laugh. I looked closer at her lips. "Mama, you can't see no more? You got lipstick above your lips!"

"Leave me alone Sharrell. Finish your work." She cut her eyes at me as I went back to my laptop and continued writing.

2012

At 184.8 pounds, I graduated with a Ph.D. in Theatre and Performance Studies in Columbia, Missouri, with my mother by my side. She worked hard to stand up out of the wheelchair to take a picture with me. She had neglected a round of chemotherapy a few weeks earlier, knowing that if she were to take it, she probably would be too sick to attend my graduation.

My mama passed/died/multiplied a month after I graduated.

I finished.

2013

July 5, 2013

196 pounds

Dear Diary,

I'm super depressed and upset. I ain't nobody's girlfriend, fiance, wifey, boo, love, ride or die chick, queen, princess, lady. Nope. None. I guess I do have low self-confidence or whatever. Why is it when a woman is man-less, they blame that on the woman? See diary, all my potentials have chosen someone else. All the dudes I used to mess wit got somebody. Robert-married, Dante-girlfriend, Ben-engaged, etc. Awe, such a depressing entry. How are you diary? With all of your positivity holding up? It's been five years since I started the weight loss program and I weigh appx. 196 pounds. Gained about 20 pounds recently. Over it!

★★★

December 31, 2013

204 pounds

Dear Diary,

Wasn't going to write but here I am. Ain't shit changed. Ready for this year to be over. Just because. I hate my weight. Ain't shit going on in Atlanta. Hate that my mama gone. Hate this fuck shit. What's wrong? My mama dead shawty! Here is my 2014 wish list:

1 lose 40 pounds
2 find one man
3 get healthier
4 save money

SAME OLE SONG

February, 2014

At 207 pounds I dialed the number to the weight loss clinic. I had no idea where the clinic was located in Los Angeles because I had recently moved to the city to begin work as an Assistant Professor of Theatre. A woman answered the phone.

"Weight Loss Clinic of Los Angeles. How may I help you?"

"Hi, I'm trying to find out where your program is located?"

"Sure. We have orientation sessions every first and third Monday. Are you interested in coming?"

"Yes."

"How'd you hear about us?"

Proudly. "I did the program a few years ago and I just need a tune-up, ya know?"

All the way across the country, I found the program that saved my life. The world premiere of "YoungGiftedandFat," the show, was coming up and I refused to get on stage at over 200 pounds. This time I didn't have the strength to do an 800-calorie diet though, so I opted for the 1200-calorie diet, which allowed me to eat a relatively healthy TV dinner. I got down to 192 pounds. I dropped out of the program after I finished my show.

★★★

May, 2015

At 206.4 pounds, I jumped out of my car and hurried into the weight loss clinic. I had re-enrolled in the 1200 calorie diet program. I have no clue as to why I can't be on time for these weight loss support meetings.

I walked up to the counter to sign in. "Hi."

"Good afternoon, Ms. Luckett."

"I'd like to purchase product and then go to the meeting."

"Sure. We just need you to weigh-in."

Shit, I thought to myself. I hate doing this every week. I went around the corner and began my weigh-in ritual. I went to the nearby restroom to empty my bladder. When I approached the scale, I removed my sneakers, earrings, and glasses. I hate doing this, I thought again. I stepped on the cold metal plate and was especially still while holding my breath. The red digital numbers read 206.4 pounds. Fuck! I don't want to go to the support group meeting anymore.

Solutions raced through my mind: call a trainer, starve myself, go on the full shake diet, never eat sugar again. A few days passed and I decided on the only option that had worked.

My phone rang from an unrecognizable number.

"Hello?"

"Hi, this is Marjorie calling from the weight loss clinic.

"Oh hi. Yes, I want to know when I can come in to enroll for the full meal replacement program because this current program isn't working. I can't stop eating." I laughed nervously.

"Sure, we have an orientation session tomorrow and another one next week."

Anxious. "How soon can I start after the orientation? I mean, I've done this before so I know the drill."

Diet. Diet. Diet. Diet. Eat food. Gain weight. Diet. Diet. Diet. Diet. Exercise. Meditate. Diet. Diet. Diet. Diet. Lose weight. Eat food. Gain Weight. Diet. Diet. Diet. Diet. I know the drill.

It is 2015 and I have gained about 30 pounds back from my lowest weight reached on the program. Yet, I'm hopeful.

The next day I sit with a handful of fat women and listen to the speech I heard nearly seven years ago.

★★★

April, 2017

At 196 pounds I typed an email to the Director of the Weight Loss Clinic in Philadelphia. I had enrolled in their partial shake/partial food program and had been driving an hour to get there every other week since I began my new assistant professor job in Pennsylvania.

> Hi Laurie,
>
> Hope this email finds you well. Unfortunately it's been a little over 2 weeks and I haven't dropped any weight. Continuing to come under these circumstances seems silly, and I guess I just need to reflect on my weight loss journey a bit more before continuing.
>
> I don't doubt I will be back sooner than later. I just need to get serious. In the meantime, can you tell me what the weekly price is to be on the full program? (This is the only option that has ever truly worked for me long term.) Thank you for your help and patience. I just need to reevaluate my goals.
>
> Sincerely,
> Sharrell

Figure 5.1: James and Beverly Luckett, mid-1980s.

STAGING LIFE

Talk "Fat" Session

> The solo black woman holds the record book inside her performance
> and inherits the griot's mission as keeper of the village history—the
> talking book—and as excavator in the genealogy of its members—all
> of us.
>
> *– D. Soyini Madison[1]*

I asked my diary how she was holding up. Who stops to think about the
well-being of the page? It holds so much information, right? The weight of
my issues, the weight of my history, my losses; they have to be held by someone or something, yes? And to ask my diary how it's doing; wow.

After my mind and body seemingly broke a part coupled with my mom
leaving me, I found myself trying to maintain my sanity and my size through
writing, and eventually through performance, as I adapted the evocative narratives found within these pages into a solo autoethnographic performance.

My autoethnographic performance serves as an analytic to further process and interrogate my various selves and my fractured world, now without
parents. I turned to embodied performance to help me connect with others
living in fat or new bodies and those who are or want to be in transition.
Performance helped me cope, and autoethnographic performance is difficult
because you are indeed revealing and sharing narratives that belong to you
and others all at once; on a vulnerable, public platform. One espouses real
life mess that has been (re)membered for public consumption and hopefully
public healing, revelations, and creation of new memories and connections.

This project pivots around processes of *writing* and *performing autoethnography*, and while a range of Performance Studies scholars, most notably Tami Spry, in her important book *Body, Paper, Stage: Writing and Performing Autoethnography*,[2] offer important directions on mapping and conceptualizing performance autoethnography, my embodied work is influenced through a theatre saturated performance studies paradigm. As explained in the introduction, this artistic choice was quite natural for me because I am a creative, and was trained in the Hendricks method, an acting methodology rooted in Black cultural traditions; a method that urges the creation of one's own work. Thus, I engaged in the process of adapting and staging my autoethnography primarily based on my existing expertise of traditional theatre training theories and methodologies. Because of my theatre training I am privy to acting and writing techniques for contemporary performance (inclusive of solo performance), improvisation, technical requirements to stage a show, and the need for production management. In addition, my training in both theatre and performance studies equipped me to explore several questions that emerged in staging this work, such as: How much of my offstage fat identity is informing the textual creation of my slender performative identity? When I write my slender voice, am I writing first through the voice of my fat self? I also considered performance of identity in relation to space. What does it mean to create a textual space in which both bodies simultaneously exist? What does it mean to have both voices speak through one organism/body? My goal was not to provide universal answers but to share one woman's attempt to suture her selves for a unified performance.

WHY A PERFORMANCE?

My solo autoethnographic performance is titled "YoungGiftedandFat." This show was birthed out of my need to merge my fat world, slender world, and liminal world; to bring together my separate lived existences. This dramatic offering transcends disciplines and borders, signaling D. Soyini Madison's reference to the Black female performing body as a "*complex mix and blend of discursive circulations, gestural economies, and historical affects that break up repetition and scatter style across hearts and minds making Black female performativity contingent, otherworldly, and radically contextual.*"[3]

The autoethnographic performance script serves as an additional intensive exploration of my performed affectations of survival as a fat Black female and a transweight female. I wholeheartedly agree with sociologist Rose Weitz who offered, "Only by looking at the embodied experiences of women, as well as how those experiences are socially constructed, can we fully understand women's lives, women's position in society, and the possibilities for resistance against that position."[4] Autoethnographic performance can indeed enact methods of resistance against the hegemonic, prejudicial status quo of body size by sharing narratives and forging moments of connection between self and other(s). This activist performative work on body size and image perception joins a long lineage of other women of the African diaspora who work(ed) to dismantle hegemonic institutions and discourses through solo performance, including some of my favorites, Beah Richards, Nina Simone, and Whoopi Goldberg.

This autoethnography and the included script is indeed a testament to the trials and tribulations of transweight women and fat women, and a call for more critical conversations about insecurities and oppression projected onto the fat body. In addition, I also consider my script a testimonial. Alluding to the history of testimonials in Latina feminist tradition, Chandra Talpade Mohanty offered that

> testimonials do not focus on the unfolding of a singular woman's consciousness (in the hegemonic tradition of European modernist autobiography); rather, their strategy is to speak *from within* a collective, as participants in revolutionary struggles, and to speak with the express purpose of bringing about social and political change.[5]

The collective from which I speak is that gathering of women, notably women of color, whose bodies narrate and tell the stories of their struggles through social constructions of their beauty, sexuality and sensuality; a collective of women who find ways to articulate their stories of fat and the fractured identities of being and becoming; struggling with acceptance that comes from the changing nature of their form and substance—finding themselves on the other side or betwixt and between themselves, sex, and society.

PRIMARY PEDAGOGICAL IMPERATIVES: AN EXEMPLAR

1) ANALYZE ADAPTATION CHOICES

"YoungGiftedandFat" is included so the reader can analyze how this autoethnography was adapted into performance autoethnography. The reader will also notice that the script includes music and movement, which allows the reader to witness the possibilities of collaboration between writer, songwriter, and choreographer, and the benefits and possible limitations of including others in the creative process. The placement of music and movement was determined by the content of the narratives and the aimed flow of the performance. As many questions will emerge about this adaptation, I hope the reader can draw their own conclusions as to why certain choices were made. The perceived answers, which may vary, might aid the reader in making decisions about staging autoethnography. This analysis may ask the reader to question the placement of narratives, and why some narratives are included in the script and some are left out. Often times the answers include time limits, how something feels, attention acts (keeping the audience engaged), and attempts at not confusing the audience.

2) Mirroring Structures

The script mirrors the structure of this book in similar ways. The reader is invited on a journey through childhood into fat youth into fat adulthood and then the aftermath of weight loss. Structures can vary. However, the mirroring structure that I utilized in creating my script proved useful because I already had a map to follow. In this way, this particular script is an example of how written autoethnographic structure can be used to inform staged autoethnographic structure.

3) Performance Studies and Theatre

By including this creative offering, I hope to make legible the benefits of having trained in both performance studies *and* traditional theatre practices. The very notion of including songs to sing and movement were influenced by my theatre training. This is not to suggest that autoethnographic performers who come to performance via performance studies are without these choices, however, being an avid reader of plays and a patron of traditional theatre (in its many forms) provides me with knowledge of the diverse structures scripts and performances can take up. In this way, having expertise in both performance studies practices *and* theatre practices expanded the ways in which I engaged in the staging process. I allowed both fields to inform my choices, animating greater possibilities of audience, cross-disciplinary collaborations, and interpretation.

*A Brief Note on Redundancy

Because "YoungGiftedandFat" is an adaptation of the previous narratives, there is redundancy in stories, however, the telling is apropos to an embodied performative paradigm. Of course this redundancy and repetition also speaks to the ebbs and flows of weight loss and how one can be at a certain weight, lose it, and then find themselves in the same spot again, but at a different moment in life, with different circumstances. I encourage you to lean into the redundant material as you investigate and analyze the choices made for adaptation.

READER'S REFLECTION #3

If you were to perform a solo show about an issue in your life, what are three possible titles of your show and why?

NOTES

1 D. Soyini Madison, "Foreword" in *solo/black/woman: Scripts, Interviews, and Essays*, ed. Patrick Johnson and Ramón Rivera-Servera (Evanston: Northwestern University Press, 2013), xiv.

2 Tami Spry, *Body, Paper, Stage: Writing and Performing Autoethnography* (Walnut Creek: Left Coast Press, 2011).

3 Madison, xiii.

4 Rose Weitz, *The Politics of Women's Bodies*, ed. Rose Weitz (New York: Oxford University Press, 2003), 10.

5 Chandra Talpade Mohanty, *Feminism Without Borders: Decolonizing Theory, Practicing Solidarity* (Durham: Duke University Press, 2003), 81.

CHAPTER 6

"YOUNGGIFTEDANDFAT"
(The Play)

© Sharrell D. Luckett & Rahbi Hines 2014

Book by Sharrell D. Luckett[1]
Lyrics by Rahbi Hines
Music by Osbaldo Maravilla

SCENE 1

(There is a cage that can be dismantled positioned upstage left. Inside the cage are green and yellowish orange vegetables, diet drink cans, a weighing scale, a jump rope, an exercise step, and an apple. The upstage part of the cage has hooks on it in which four to six of Sharrell's wigs are hanging. This cage represents perfection for Sharrell. Upstage right is a staircase. There is a bottle of orange diet Sunkist soda and potato chips slightly hidden under the staircase. Attached to the staircase is a picture of Sharrell's mother. Hanging from a downstage batten is a fast food chain burger bag with a sandwich in it. On the upstage back wall is a projection area where oversized white and beige clothes are pinned together to make a projection screen. Quotes, thoughts, and images are displayed on the clothing projection screen. Pinned to the walls are very large sized women's clothes. There are three movable black boxes on the stage as well. Lights up on SHARRELL. She enters from the audience dressed in a baby doll dress and is wearing a wig styled in two child-like ponytails with ribbons.[2])

SHARRELL: Feast your eyes on me. Knock-kneed, pigeon-toed dame. One leg may actually be longer than the other. My arms reach out to 27 inches and the fatty deposits hang ever so nicely. *(She shakes the fat on her arms.)* Jiggle, jiggle, jiggle. My belly hangs over my thighs and I cannot see my parts. In dance class when I try to turn out, my feet only point straight forward. My booty has four lumps. Let's count them: one, two, three, four. My back is covered in heavy rolls, and there are stretchmarks all over my body taking you anywhere you would like to go. I camouflage the flat back of my head with two ponytails. My best angle is my side.

(She poses four times and then retreats to the cage when she notices the dangling burger bag.)

I take pride in my jawline and when I think dudes are looking I elongate my fat, rolled neck to show off the only skinny part of my body. Lastly, there are moles all over my face and neck; three on my left cheek and moles all around my mouth. *(She smiles.)* Pearly white teeth. *(Sharrell fixates on the burger bag.)*

SONG 1: "HUNGRY"

SHARRELL: Hungry, why am I always hungry?
All I long for is beauty, a new me, a slim me
So hungry, uhhhh, ummmm
Why am I always hungry?
Two helpings of perfection is no fun
False freedom for everyone

(As Sharrell gives in to temptation for the food in the burger bag, she steps out of the cage and runs over to the bag. She goes back and forth in her mind trying to fight her food desires. Finally, she opens the bag and takes a bite of the burger. While chewing the burger Sharrell becomes entranced by the delicious grease and begins a sensual food DANCE. The dance highlights Sharrell and her love of food. Sharrell eventually comes out of the trance dance and throws the sandwich and bag onto the floor.)

Constantly monitoring, I can't take it
Diet to diet to diet, Yeah I break it
Send him a pic from the side and just fake it
Over it, I'm over it!
The party's tonight, I have nothing to wear
Who is this girl that I see in the mirror?
End it today or just live in fear?
Over it, I'm over it!
And hungry, why am I always hungry?
All I long for is beauty, a new me, a slim me
So hungry, uhhhh, ummmm

END SONG

128

(While a voiceover of Sharrell's mother begins to play, Sharrell retreats to the cage and retrieves the apple.)

MOTHER'S VOICEOVER: When you were about nine years old I believe that was when I started realizing I had to buy a little larger sizes for you and I didn't see it as a real problem at the time and actually I've never felt it was a real problem for me. But as you began in your tween years and then your teen years, uh with the mockings and harassment by classmates and neighborhood kids, I realized that it was a problem, a big problem for you. And of course since it affected you, it affected me because you were a beautiful little girl with pretty hair, beautiful skin, and I really didn't understand it. It really upset me that, when you would be the victim of meanness, and you know of course there were situations where you retaliated and quite a few kids got beat up. *(End Voiceover.)*

SHARRELL: They say apples are good for your teeth, a natural flosser or something like that. That's all I used to get compliments on when I was little. It was all of my mama's friends. They would talk about my white teeth and my nice skin. *(Singing.)* Ooooh Beverly take a look at her white teeth, nice skin, white teeth, nice skin, white teeth, nice skin, ooooh Beverly. *(End singing.)* That's it, that's all. My mama would just smile and thank them. But me, I didn't care either way. Cuz I knew that my white teeth and my nice skin did not make me beautiful, not beautiful like my mama at least. My mama, she was where all the confusion began. I was in kindergarten when a classmate hipped me to the fact that you are sposed to look like yo mama. My mama was beau-ti-ful, hot, sizzling, fierce. When she walked into those Parent Teacher Association meetings the room would just stop, cuz everybody was in awe of her beauty. And she would have her long hair flowing down her back, which I later learned was weave, she was way ahead of the weave explosion. And the next day at school, all the kids would talk about how pretty my mama was. They would say, "Oooh Sharrell yo mama so pretty. Oooooooh Sharrell yo mama so pretty!" And I would just smile until one day this girl said, "Oooh Sharrell your mama is so pretty …" *(Sharrell crosses upstage to get the picture of her mother.)* "… why don't you look like her?" *(Sharrell hands the picture to an audience member and asks her/him to pass it around. Sharrell then goes upstage and takes a long drink of the orange diet Sunkist soda.)*

Why don't I look like her? I didn't understand the question. My young mind didn't understand the question. I didn't even know I was sposed to look like my mama. And if my mama is pretty and I don't look like her, then what does that make me? If my mama is pretty, and I don't look like her, then what am I?

(Pause.)

My mama. Isn't she gorgeous? I could never amount to her. At age 15, I was far from fine. In fact, I had no semblance of beauty that I should have inherited from my parents. My father loved the finer things in life, women at the top of the list. My mama could be likened to a swan. She was tall and thin with chiseled cheek bones and bedroom eyes. In her younger days, she was often compared to Beverly Johnson, the first Black super model to grace the cover of *Vogue*, circa 1974. Now my daddy was the Paul Robeson/Denzel Washington/Shaft of his day. He had the build of a slender football player, a deep baritone singing voice, was a gifted mathematician, and excelled in track and field. At 6'2" my daddy could talk any woman out of her drawers with his sparkling white smile and broad shoulders. Together, my picturesque parents were often identified as a Hollywood couple in which the stranger "Couldn't figure out who they were, but if we gave her a few seconds, she would have the answer." I have vivid memories of walking with my mama and hearing men whistle. They would just be whistling and my mama would be smiling, but she really didn't pay them any mind cuz she already had her a husband. And together, you would think this striking couple would make heaven, instead they made Sharrell.

(A kiddy/childish/playful musical tune is heard. Sharrell retrieves the photo from the audience and tapes it back to the staircase. She begins to run around as if she is playing with other children.)

SCENE 2

SHARRELL: Dudes will fundamentally rearrange your existence
I got pissed on when I was five, that lil boy was live
rolling down the street on his big wheel
he was cute and decided to take a feel on
my little Black body
and it felt good, it felt real good
He excited me like a real man should but
he was four and a half and I was five

and somewhere in between the hunching and kissing
my first kiss I remember it so well
his teeth knocked against mine and till this day I remember what
his lil boy baby breath smelt like, brand new
And his daddy was hot and I was not
ready for the porn magazines strewn across the bedroom floor, at
 age five
white women pussy galore and we argued
(Sharrell acts like the little boy and herself.)
Him: That's what you look like!
Sharrell: Uh uhn.
Him: Uh huh!
Sharrell: No I don't. I don't look like that!
Him: You will!
And we hunched every second we could!
Mama, I'm going out to play. *(She hunches.)* Mama, I'm going out
 to play. *(She hunches.)* Mama, I'm going out to play. *(She runs and*
 hunches and then crosses to the downstage edge of the stage.) Clothes
 always on, still felt good
I remember it, so nasty, why was these women so trashy, these porns?
But my interest was piqued
and me and him kept feeling on each other and
hunching
It was the best, till I found out he was messin' with all the other little
 girls in the neighborhood
nonetheless I was hot, sprung, and gushing
always needed my fix
always needed my male friends
I grew taller and bigger, he stayed short and thin
We got caught eventually
my mama made me promise not to give him no more
and I said OK mama as I flew out that door
still tell lies like I did before
needed my fix, 'bout age ten
He said let's play house, I knew what that meant
I threw my legs up into the air as he announced, "Honey I'm home
 from work."

and as the TV had so wonderfully taught me, I let him lay in between
  my legs and we got to hunching and I wasn't thinking 'bout my
  mama no more, cuz that boy felt good,
and then I seent her
Shit! She was peeping out the kitchen window and she called me in.
  (Imitating Mama.) "Sharrell!!!!!"
My mama beat my ass.
She beat me so bad that I fell into the closet and broke it and she
  would not stop beating me.
He ran home, I was screaming, he was running, I was screaming
and all I thought after she finished beating my ass was
I guess I can't do that kind of stuff in public no more
So my sexuality became my secret
My youthful orgasms became my secret
My young hotness became my secret, and you know the funny thing
  about secrets is, I just can't keep 'em
I don't know how to wrap stuff up tight and protect it and not
  tell nobody
And somewhere between nine and ten, when me and Kyree started
  to be just friends,
I got fat and "it" wasn't fun no more
Something went way wrong and I ended up fat
And what made it worse is that dudes don't like fat girls. They don't.
And I found that out at an early age cuz none of them wanted to feel
  on me when I got fat
The fatness just ripped my childhood into pieces
And I don't know if me and Kyree stopped feeling on each other
  cuz I got fat or if because I got fat, I stopped messing around. I
  don't know.
I just know that the boys didn't wanna play "hide and go get" no
  more, you know "hide and go get," the alternative version of "hide
  and seek," but when they find you they get "it," but none of the
  boys wanted it
and my brother tried to intervene
even told the boys to chase me
got them to agree that when he counted to three they would chase me
but even after they agreed they dodged me
and tackled cute, little light-skinned Rasheeda Baity,

a cute lil girl wit two ponytails who giggled as she and the five
   boys fell
to the ground in excitement as I stood
painfully aware that no boys desired to chase me
(*Pause*)

I thought everybody got orgasms. I thought all little kids felt on each other.
I mean, it's normal. It's normal right? Being so young and so, I don't know,
hot? I mean they say babies masturbate in the womb. My mama used to
think I was molested but I don't have any crazy memories of grown folks
touching me. I think I'm pretty normal. Do you know what it feels like to
be sexual, to feel sexual, and nobody wants it, I mean nobody?

Song 2: "Good 'N Plenty"

Excuse me, would you like to try a little piece of heaven?
Peach, cherry, strawberry, uhh hurry cause it's melting
Try my new flavor cause I ran out of skinny
And you've been here before so I know you like good and plenty
You're leaving?
Noooooooooooooo

END SONG

I could sell orgasms on the corner like people sell lemonade!

Projection 1:

33% to 50% of women experience orgasm infrequently

Have my little orgasm sell going on, probably charge ten cents or something
cuz I got so many to give away.

Projection 2:

90% of orgasm problems appear to be psychological in nature

I'm not crazy.

SCENE 3

SHARRELL: When I was 11, this teenage boy threatened to shoot me because I was fat. He threatened me as I walked past his house. Didn't even know me and said he was gonna shoot me cuz I was fat. I later found out that he really had a gun. Good thing I kept walking. *(Sharrell crosses center stage.)* The worst thing that happened to me cuz I was fat happened in middle school. By the time I was in middle school I had developed a little mouth. I would curse around the teachers and stuff and finally the teachers got tired of me cursing and I got out-of-school suspension for four days. Around this same time, my mama became real religious, like religious stupid, like you know how religious folks get in that stage where just because they meet somebody else who loves Jesus they assume that person is cool? Well my mama ran into a lady who was a preacher and somewhere in their conversation my mama told the preacher I was suspended and the preacher told my mama that her daughter got out-of-school suspension too. And these God-fearing women who had just met, decided it was a good idea for me and the girl to spend our out-of-school suspension time together. Bad parenting moment. I was like 13 and she was like 15. So when I got to the girl's house she was like, "What you do?" And you know I was like, "I cursed, you know I cursed." And then I was like, "What you do?" And she was like, "I brought a gun to school." *(Sharrell's mouth flies open.)* And I was in shock but trying not to show it and was thinking mama what in the hell have you done? And you know texting didn't exist and I couldn't get in touch with my mama. I was stuck. The next day the girl's mama went to work and left us at home. And the girl did what all teenagers do when they're left at home unsupervised. She invited some dudes over. Mike and Dante. Mike was hers and Dante was supposed to be for me, but me and little Dante just sat at opposite ends of the room, quiet, not talking. Then Mike started teasing Dante and was like "Dante, wussup? You was talking all that junk, talking bout you gone be all over Sharrell and doing this, that, and the other to her. Wussup? Why you so quiet?" And Mike laughed and the girl giggled and Dante was smirking. And I tried to laugh too, tried to act like it was all good but we all knew that Dante wasn't messing with me cuz he thought I was fat and ugly. Then I tried to divert the attention away from me and I asked Mike laughingly, "Why you so crazy?" And then I realized Mike really was crazy. He started jumping up and down, up and down, up and down, and was like "I ain't crazy, I ain't crazy," and I kept laughing, cuz I'm thinking he cool, you know, cuz he laughing. Then Mike reached down and picked up a glass vase off the coffee table. It was big and had water and beautiful flowers in it and he threw it at me as hard as he could. The vase hit my upper left chest and shattered from the impact. Water was all over my shirt and I didn't know what to do. Then Mike was standing over me, breathing real hard. He had one hand bawled up in a fist and the other behind his back. And I was scared and I noticed Dante was scared and Dante was like, "Mike, don't do it man, don't do it man, Mike don't do it." And Dante kept repeating that until Mike stormed out of the house. Dante ran out behind him. And the girl who brought a gun to school jumped on the floor and started cleaning up the glass. She said, "You can't tell nobody, my mama can't find out. If you tell, I swear I'll kill you." *(Sharrell crosses upstage towards the cage and removes her wig.)* And she did.

(Music begins to play and slightly changes the mood. Sharrell dances out of her baby doll dress into "too big" clothes. Her real hair is messy and uncombed. She looks disheveled. A school bell rings.)

Then came high school.

Song 3: "Rejection"

I remember what it was like in high school
Nobody, no one liked me

I was in the drama program it was a bunch of us, we were like family

Nobody, no one liked me

And by this time, I had learned the hard lessons about fatness as it relates to boys

No one liked me

I was a mess. And it didn't help that I went to school with all of these

Pretty girls
Nobody, no one liked me
and the boys and the teacher were always telling them
Oh you so cute, oh you so fine, ooooh you so gorgeous, look at her eyes

Look at her eyes, what about mine, don't you think I'm fine, you just
tryna hate
Huh, it's my weight?

The boys just seemed to like everybody but me, and when I did ask my
friends why the dudes didn't compliment me, they all gave the same answer:
"You don't *look* like you need that kind of attention Sharrell."

I remember what it was like in high school, nobody, no one liked me
And when I, when I walked in the lunchroom, nobody sat beside me
They only pointed, they only stared
I was scared, started running around
I was scared, self-esteem on the ground
I couldn't take it
I didn't like it

The first time I got a compliment in high school I was in the 10th grade
putting on lipstick cuz I was in a show and this girl said, "Ooooh, Sharrell
you got pretty lips." Then a few years later this girl saw me with my glasses
off and she said, "You have nice eyes." Pretty lips, nice eyes, whatever.

They only pointed they only stared
I was scared, started running around
I was scared, self-esteem on the ground
I couldn't take it I didn't like it
Wish I could blink my eyes and then be outta sight, outta sight, outta
sight, outta sight

END SONG

SHARRELL: When I was a child I would close my eyes and really believe
that I was invisible. Just stand up against a wall in broad daylight and black
out. Now you see me, now you don't. The darkness became so familiar. And
at my lowest point in life, I would make myself invisible so frequently that
I forgot how to use my light. Searching the darkness with my fingers, pulse,
my breath, and my eyes, darting from one crevice to the next. No light
switches anywhere, so I adapted to the darkness. Made a big comfy bed in it
and slept in it every night. Face wet and salty and supple. Drowning in the

black abyss. In deep, no longer searching for switches or motion-activated lights. In the coastal south, you're supposed to stock up on candles and flashlights for hurricane season. My mama was always good about that. She put a flashlight and a candle in every room in the house, and when it started to thunder and lightning really bad my mama walked fast through the house, lighting the candles, preparing us for the storm. But she couldn't figure out how to light the candles during my storm. And by the time I was a teenager all of the batteries in the flashlights had run out. So my mama would just sit with me in the darkness and change the wet pillowcases and assure me that the only reason I knew it was dark was because I have experienced my light.

Scene 4

SHARRELL: I was in undergrad auditioning for some short plays when I met Robert. I guess he thought my fat body and loud mouth were perfect for the role of this 60-year-old woman in his one-act play. I was 19. Robert and I both wore glasses. He was thin, quiet, inquisitive, a writer. My guard was completely down so it was nothing to try and be his friend. We hung out and little by little his quietness made me curious about him. He ended up directing me in his play, and continued to direct me in life for the next five years I guess you could say. I hung on to his every word and thought he knew everything. He was my first real love and managed to make me somewhat happy. We could talk for hours on end. Even started a musical group. The new Digable Planets. He warned me about my selfishness and I constantly scolded him for being a perfectionist. We were the perfect, unperfect couple. I thought our arguments were healthy and he thought relationships should be easier. We clung to one another. He loved me, in a real way, and didn't like the fact that I had issues loving myself, so he was often pointing out my good qualities. With every kiss he was chipping away at my hard exterior. It was my friend who asked me when Robert and I were getting married. I hadn't even thought about it. Marriage seemed boring to me. I'd much rather stay in boyfriend, girlfriend stage. Five long years.

(Simulating a phone conversation with a friend.)

Hello. Nothing. I'm not always depressed. Robert won't talk to me. He acting like he don't love me no more. I just thought we was gone be together forever, have babies. Where you wanna go? No. I don't wanna go. No, cuz I don't like the club. Dudes don't talk to me. No they won't. They never look at me. What you wearing? Alright, alright Ima throw something on. I'll be ready in bout 20 minutes. *(End phone conversation.)*

I got up and got dressed. It was time to leave. I decided to take one last approving look at myself in the mirror. I looked hot, like all fat people looked to me: hot and swollen and greasy and sad. I had gained about 30 pounds after breaking up with Robert. Maybe it's because I found his e-mail.

(Simulating a phone conversation with a friend.)

Hello, I'm not going. Because I don't like my outfit and I'm sleepy.

(End phone conversation.)

We hung up. My fat reflection had finally overpowered me. Maybe my ex-boyfriend was right about me in that e-mail, maybe I am special. After Robert and I broke up, after a long five years in a relationship, I would canvass his e-mails to see what was going on in his life, who he was dating, and one day I came across this e-mail. He had a friend who was trying to hook him up with another girl and his response to his friend ... *(Sharrell's voice trails off.)*

Projection 3:

Yeah, I actually did find your friend online. Umm, don't think I'm interested though. I know you think I'll mess with anybody based on how Sharrell looked. But you have to realize that was a special circumstance. Definitely not putting your friend in her category, but I'll pass for now.

SHARRELL: There will now be a five minute depression.

(The projection becomes distorted and Sharrell enters a deep depression. She then exits the stage while footage of her intense depression is shown.)

Scene 5

SHARRELL: *(She enters through the audience.)* I arrived at the weight loss clinic in an attempt to right what had been wrong all of my life. I felt like the shake diet was my last option. I had been eating a little less over the last week to prepare me for the 800-calorie diet that loomed ahead for the next four months. The beige walls resembled any other medical office. The receptionists wore mosaic swirly dark blue and white ascots, complemented with a navy blazer and white blouse. It was quiet. I was surrounded by other big bodies that I assumed would be my weight loss cohort. As I sifted through the pages of the usual waiting room magazines, my mind was blank. I had no further opinion about whether or not I should try this low-calorie diet and risk further humiliation from my family and friends if I failed. I was here because I needed to be in order to survive in this backwards world. Moments later, I was whisked away to begin my enrollment *(She runs upstage.)* The nurse pointed me in the direction of the scale at the end of the hallway. I wished I had access to a sort of "last meal" at this moment. Walking down that hallway was like being on death row walking to my execution. The scale was big enough to hold six people at once, but I had to go at it alone. After the scale confirmed that I was morbidly obese, weighing in at close to 300 pounds, I was asked to stand in front of a blank wall so they could take a picture of me. This "before" picture stood for everything at that moment: for my sanity, for the many men who ignored me, for my morbidly obese aunts, for my hundreds of tear-filled nights, for my right to be thin, and for my father, who I felt was ashamed of me.

MOTHER'S VOICEOVER: Your daddy would comment about both of his girls, and uh he said Sharrell is gonna have hips like this and he puts his hands in a curvature mode and she's gonna be fine, oooh. You wanted your father to be proud of you. Cuz you loved your daddy and daddy was forgiven and daddy was sweet daddy. *(End Voiceover.)*

SHARRELL: And with the flash of the camera, the last known photo of fat Sharrell was taken.

Projection 4:

-10 pounds, -16 pounds, -25 pounds, -32 pounds,
-40 pounds, -45 pounds, -55 pounds,
-70 pounds, -78 pounds, -95 pounds

SHARRELL: I stopped eating and one morning I woke up and couldn't fit any of my clothes. I stopped eating and one morning I woke up and couldn't find myself. I stopped eating and one morning I woke up and was happy. And the happiness wouldn't go away. Everything was too big; no I was too small! I had no idea that thin privilege existed. Yes, small people have it really, really good. The same year that I lost weight, the stage was set for new beginnings in so many ways. I decided to go to graduate school for theatre. Off to Missouri I went. A new place, new people, new expectations. No one knew my history, so I could "pass" as someone who I was not. I read somewhere that "the possibility of passing, trying to lose weight, wanting to become 'normal,' is about the only recognized option available to fat women." Once I got to grad school as this new person, I decided to audition for a play, the world premiere of *Holding Up the Sky*. This play only had two leading roles; a beautiful, young, vibrant husband and wife. The play also had ensemble roles, and naturally I gravitated towards the ensemble roles because that is what I was usually cast in as a fat girl. On the day of auditions I wore basic black. After performing my monologue with intensity and dramatic flair, the director informed me that he wanted me to read for a certain part. When I looked down at the script, I saw the lines for the gorgeous, elegant, sexy leading lady. My heart started racing because surely he had made a mistake! (*Pause*) I was confused and anxious. In my mind I didn't fit the role. This character was supposed to be beautiful and believably desirable. I had never been asked to play a feminine, beautiful lead and I wasn't sure I could believably accomplish femininity during the audition. See fat women are not taught how to be feminine. Little fat girls are not encouraged to cross their legs, or watch out for the boys. People are less concerned with whether or not they eat with their mouths closed. Little fat girls are not allowed to cry. They are not made to feel like their bodies are worthy of protection. Little fat girls become fat women who are unloved. Still, when reading for the role in front of the director I used my imagination in a way that I'd never done before. I implemented what I thought were feminine gestures and made sure that my long braids were flowing down my back. I walked daintily across the floor and imagined myself to be thin, thin, thin, thin. Later that week, I received an e-mail that I, Sharrell Luckett, had been cast as the sexy, beautiful leading lady. I was elated until I realized that I had to make sure and keep the weight off. We began rehearsals in October, there was a show in November, and then I had to make it through Thanksgiving and Christmas in order to perform the show again in late January. Awe hell! The odds were against me. It's said that only five percent of people who lose weight on a rapid weight loss diet will keep the weight off. To make matters worse, I discovered that I had to be damn near naked, wearing a scantily clad costume, be lifted by my husband, and simulate having sex onstage with an orgasm. I was scared. How was I going to pull this off? The answer was simple. I had to believe in myself.

Projection 5:

(A video clip of Sharrell performing as the "Young Woman" in Holding Up the Sky. *The following voiceover plays concurrently with the footage.)*

Voiceover—Interview with the Director

SHARRELL: Before you met me tell me what you thought about the physicality that the "Young Woman" needed to possess.

DIRECTOR: I was looking for that sense of body consciousness that says I'm comfortable in my own skin because I don't have anything to compare myself to because I'm the first woman. So there is no judgment as to whether or not I'm worthy, unworthy, desirable, undesirable. I'm fully confident because I'm the only one. I am. I'm here and I am woman. The only one and the first one. A woman who presents herself with no apologies and no judgments.

SHARRELL: So, when you just described this young woman that you would pull out of the ground, physically was I bigger than that, was I smaller than that?

DIRECTOR: No. You are just about right.

SHARRELL: Okay.

DIRECTOR: If you were bigger, I probably would not have [cast you] … I'll say that. *(This line repeats. End voiceover. Music with a lighter, sexy feel is played.)*

SHARRELL: When I lost weight my life got better in the blink of an eye. Suddenly I was pretty, sexy, a bitch for no reason, and I could finally own up to my robust sexuality. Men were coming out of the woodwork, old, young, and younger. My friend in Missouri told me that these dudes admitted that I make them sweat, that I made them go to church and pray real hard for strength so they wouldn't cheat on their fiancés with me. Men finally liked me … and I liked them too!

Scene 6

SHARRELL: But I wasn't used to all these dick-stractions. You mean now I can have any dude I want? That's what my friend said: "Sharrell, you can have any dude you want!" And I believe it! But sometimes the wrong ones find me; you know, the married ones, the engaged ones, the just separated ones, the ones in relationships with several women. But if they smart and cute, I just can't resist. *(Pause.)*

> Look at you skinny
> Got me wide open and hot like a pot uv grits
> Now I'm getting served
> Bubbling brown hot dog sticks
> Too many
> I ain't got enough holes
> They all won't fit; don't make me choose
> dumb decisions; I ain't used to this
> abuse is bliss
> is this what dem thin bitches be complainin about?
> count me in; let em out
> pass the cuties but save the cooties
> wink at the married ones cuz they smoking guns
> ready to burst, pop, spazz at any second
> shawty swang my way, I'll be ur second blessing
> dumb decisions; more pregnancy tests in one month
> than I'm used to
> I'm rolling my third blunt; all thanks to my cuteness
> Yeah, I'm loose and I think I'm losin'
> I ain't used to this
> Fullness; all wrapped up in his arms
> Don't mind if he's an alcoholic
> Cuz he, he be my daddy
> Remind me of my daddy
> That's a shame; rolling blunts with my daddy
> Sexing up his frame
> Drowning in a spa full of cold water
> Posin' for a pic that's gon' take me under
> I swear I'll let him go if you promise to love me
> When he leaves
> Wither up and get offa me; I gotta go to school
> Big ambitions and a lot of talk
> But dem mens make me fall
> I asked God to send me a sign

I'm layin' on my back just taking it
I wish she'd call
I swear I'll pick up and suck the milk from her breasts
Even share my eggs cuz motherhood I missed
Now skinny has got me wide open
Legs stretched and I'm hoping
Something good will come out of this Whipped cream rushing
All this like has got me blushing
I'm wishing that love would visit me at any second
I don't think that thang can find me
I told that trick I'm in the red light district
And they hitting it
Standing under the lamp post; slightly twitching
My lips ain't in alignment
Face down in the water
I hear laughter; reminds me of my pastor
That I never had
So my mind grazes in the pasture of my past
I draw blanks
Just like he do
Throw daggers with my eyes
Just like she do
And I laugh
cuz all this like is something I ain't never had
(*Pause*)

SHARRELL: When I was fat, I could not comb my hair, throw on a hoodie with some tennis shoes, and nobody would talk to me. But now, I can do the same thang, and some man gone be flirting with me. I can't hide no more. And since I was fat and dudes didn't talk to me I missed out on the whole dating scene. Like, I don't know how to talk to dudes. I don't know when they're flirting. I was just thrown into a whole new world that my fat mind could not comprehend. Even though my body was smaller, my mind was having trouble keeping up, especially on the dating scene. Rule after rule after rule after rule, I did not know. So my friends sat me down and helped me out, especially when they saw I was making bad decisions. "Ok Sharrell, listen:"

1   You do not have to give your real number to a dude when he asks for it.

2   When a dude says "yo shawty whatsup," ignore him and keep walking.

3   Do not go back to the hotel with a dude unless ur going to fuck him; he does not want to talk.

4   Don't go over the dude's house on the first date.

5   If a dude tells you he usually doesn't date dark-skinned girls, but you're an exception, do not continue to talk to him and text him afterwards.

6   Do not for any reason tell your girlfriends who you like cuz they will surely screw him behind your back.

(Pause)

All of these rules that I should've known by the time I was 28, that I missed out on cuz I wasn't able to date. And then me tryna keep my weight down, not letting on that I was living a great big ole lie, that I had a huge secret, started stressing me out. So whenever a dude would show interest, at some point I felt like I needed to "come out" to him.

(Sharrell pretends she is speaking to a man.) Sit down. I have something to tell you. OK, promise you won't make a face and promise you won't get mad. Just don't say nothing. *(Deep breath.)* I used to be fat. *(A very long pause.)* And it's this moment that surprises me. It surprises me so much that I should keep the damn secret to myself, cuz the dudes always be like, "OK." One after the other, I told the dudes I used to be fat and it always seemed like they didn't care or it didn't phase them, and I'm flabbergasted. But see the real reason I'm telling them is cuz this slenderness ain't me and as we all know I can get fat, plump, big, at any second. I gain weight like that. It's so hard to live a secret and try to give people, men, I should say, what you think they want, what you know they want, cuz I know that every dude I've messed with since I've lost weight, wouldn't have messed with me if I were fat. In the meantime, I'm going to take advantage of being smaller. The world is so nice to small people. People smile at me for no reason. I can fit on the airplanes. I can sit on the rollercoasters. I get invited more places. No one looks at me when I get a second helping of food. No one stares at me while I'm eating, and I can shop basically anywhere. *(Pause.)* And I want it. All of the niceness. So I go to the gym non-stop all day everyday to keep the weight off, and I was doing great till I came home from graduate school.

SCENE 7

SHARRELL: I met this dude who could cook and I liked him and I think he liked me, and by this time I had kept the weight off for about three and a half years and here he comes, a damn chef. So there I was eating my little heart out. And I just got so lost in him that I didn't realize he was a dog, but I couldn't get out. And my mama, I think she was just happy for me and was trying to let me figure this thing called "skinny" out. She just wanted me to be happy, and she was real proud of me and I was real proud cuz by this point I had *had* several cute dudes and she had met some of them and I was happy and she was happy and I was happy and he was a dog. But I was happy that I had a man who would get mad if he thought I had another man. And I was happy that somebody cared whether or not I was cheating. And he was happy to be seeing several women at the same time and I was happy to be one of them, cuz I had convinced myself that I would never have a man. And my mama was happy cuz I was happy, then my mama was sick, suddenly she was sick. *(Pause.)* My mama was my best friend. She didn't shy away from sexuality. She knew. She knew I had this robust hotness so she would talk openly about sex to me and when I got old enough she would probe in her motherly way. *(Sharrell pretends to have a conversation with her mother.)*

SHARRELL AS HER MAMA: "Did you like him? How big was it?"

SHARRELL: "Mama!"

SHARRELL AS HER MAMA: " I just wanted to know. He don't look like he got nothing … but you know yo daddy …"

SHARRELL: "Mama, you bout to gross me out! And I am not talking about my dude's thang with you." And I revert back to childhood. "We ain't doing nothing, we don't have sex." All of 28 and shit. *(End conversation.)*

SHARRELL: My mama, the woman who

Birthed me

Wrote a book before me, married God, performed before me

Beat me when I was trying to screw in elementary school

Beat me again when I wouldn't stop trying

Yelled at my daddy when he messed up

Stayed with my daddy when he messed up

Bought me McDonald's every time I asked

Showed me how to cut up bed sheets to use them as maxipads for hard times

Introduced me to Jesus at age 11

Smelled me after I snuck out the house at age 14 to go be with a boy

Caught me talking nasty on the phone, though she listened for three minutes before interrupting

And bought me diet orange Sunkist soda on the first day of my diet

(Sharrell drinks diet orange Sunkist soda.)

PROJECTION 6:

(Silent footage is shown of Sharrell's mother giving an impromptu sermon in her kitchen. She is talking, laughing, and smiling at the camera. This footage is followed by a silent reflection during which Sharrell does a DANCE of acceptance.)

SCENE 8

(Throughout this scene Sharrell slowly dismantles the cage.)

Father of Black back

Mother of strong bones

Consecrated in the middle to create my song

Within me, his wit

The curve of his smile

pearly white teeth

legs that run for miles

Not to mention my mathematical genius

Goes unused

But who needs chemistry when u've got the blues?

Too much pressure

In the crock pot

To be like her: hot

From Jane Eyre to Elizabeth Taylor,

From Beverly Johnson to a fine Black woman, just name her

Nothing like her

The woman who bore me pain

Nothing like, yet identical all the same

A thing for men who didn't love me back

A thing for boys that scolded my fat

These rolls on my back

This meat on my thigh

cut it off and it'll stand a mile high

Big, Black, bitch
That was my name
Big, Black, bitch
The little niggas would all proclaim
Threw me into silence
Forced me into shame
Ran from me while playing
"take yo fat friend home"
"take yo fat friend home" and don't bring her back the next day
I think those boys made me hide my song
The world made me hide my song
My song
I'm not singing it yet
It's tucked away somewhere
Catching its breath
Been running far too long
Hiding under clothes too small
Under hate that's well worn
Under burgundy rivers that sleep in my womb
In feathers of the pillow that catch my tears released too soon
In long-awaited nights
In all my years
My song transcends my fears
Beah Richards says
A Black woman speaks
About oppression, about slavery, about all this heat
Fuck those little black niggas and these grown men
That withheld their drooling
Down with skinny bitches and all this schooling
Fuck a scale
Fuck a diet
Fuck fruits and vegetables
This is my riot
And although I open my mouth
My song won't come out
It sits in silence
I am a Black woman who wishes for a time

That I could gain my weight back
And still be fine
That I can let my curly hair show and blow in the wind
Without being seen as a threat to all men
So I wear straight wigs
This degree that flows down my back; I want it for all my Black people
that have been attacked
All of my niggas that's been held back
I read and write and read and fight
Read and write and read and cry
Read and write, and when I speak—fly
Bag lady, why you carrying all them bags?
I carry them to remind me of my past
All the "no you can'ts" all of the "you're too bigs"
All of the "why you so Black and yo mama light-skinned?"
All of the "you won't get a jobs" all of the "they won't let you ins"
All of the "you can't ever be a teacher cuz you distract the kids"
I wish I could fall into the arms of my father and do it all again
I'd whisper in his ear, that he's a great man
I'd tell him to keep his sperm
Locked away in his pants
but I guess my mama felt too good and the universe decided to give me
a chance
So here I am.
My mama wrote a book ten years ago, I couldn't even get off page three
Still trying to figure out what exactly a dissertation is
How many chapters, tell me again?
Cuz it's not enough
And on top of that we don't even speak the same language
I can't possibly FIT my story
Within yo structure
If I let you in my world
you will melt like a popsicle shoved in the mouths of babes
I just learned how to read and write yesterday and now you want me to
write a book
OK, I'll write

but you're gonna need to go to Africa and China when I'm done and
find a translator
cuz the space in between the lines is my incubator
My brain will not sit on a shelf at any institution that says
February is "nigger month"
and invites Dr. Angelou for restitution
And even if that ain't the way it went you shoulda canceled her contract
and told her to save her two cents; besides talking ain't neva did shit
I say we burn down this bitch
But wait, wait, not before I graduate
Not before I walk across that stage
I'm doing this for my mama, just so she can say
My daughter Sharrell has got her Ph.D.
And after that I will throw that diploma in the murky sea
Cuz these fictions of theory and history do not define me
What exactly is a dissertation again?
I'm still confused
Who needs an education when u've got the blues?
I'm told the dissertation is a gap in time
Really?
Like the time Black men are doing in prison for smoking weed?
Or the time lines in the history book that don't include me?
No, no, a gap in time like this space between my two front teeth?
Like this space between you and me?
Maybe that's why I'm classified as morbidly obese
Maybe that's why I'm hungry right now
Fat and hungry as ever so feed me
I'm hungry like I've never been before
I want some white chocolate ice cream
even though I came through the back door
To tear down the master's house, one must use the master's tools?
Well here I am sitting in your school
Sitting in silence and it tastes so good
Everything I need to know, I actually learn in the hood
Full of Black babies dangling on the edge of humanity
I gotta go home cuz somebody's calling out for me
I went missing in 2008; shed my skin; withered away

This body ain't mine; it never belonged to me
Escaped like a thief in the night
And I'm trying to find me with all my might
What is this in my hand?
What is this in my hand?
If you force me to speak, I will surely tell a lie
When I killed myself I had an alibi
I was at home alone
Wanting to be let out
I had to find my song
And now my ancestors tell me, it's been within me all along
So why, in God's name, am I so far from home?
A skinny bitch could never do this shit
That fat Black girl sings my song.

Song 4: "Shedding"

Nobody said the road you travel would be easy
And often times we have to learn the hard way
But in the end you realize that all your trials
Have come along to form the words of your life song
Oh oh oh, in life I always thought that I'd never make it cuz I'm
too big
So afraid of what I saw, tried to do everything to change it
Took awhile for me to see that everything I had is what I needed
Oh I am young, Black, and gifted
Oh I am young, Black, and gifted
I remember when he held me in the winter
But when the sun came he up and went away
Now I look to the sky and know that I'm amazing
Smile and thank God for making me this way
Oh, oh, oh, I'm done with lonely nights
Of crying in the dark when love is needed
And I'm standing in my light
Can hear my mother say keep on believing
Took a while for me to see that everything I had is what I needed
Oh I am young, Black, and gifted
Oh I am young, Black, and gifted

I'm flying away from all of the tears and all the pain
Running towards a better day
Loving myself, reclaiming me
Took awhile for me to see that everything I had is what I needed
Oh I am young, Black, and gifted
Oh I am young, Black, and gifted
Oh I am young, Black, fat, and gifted

END SONG

BLACK OUT

Figure 6.1: Sharrell as herself in "YoungGiftedandFat."

NOTES

1 "YoungGiftedandFat" premiered in June of 2014 at California State University,-Dominguez Hills in Carson, CA. It was directed by Freddie Hendricks; the musical director and lyricist was Rahbi Hines, the choreographer and media designer was Guy Thorne, the composer was Osbaldo Maravilla, the set design was by Evan Bartoletti, the costume design was by Carin Jacobs, the lighting design was by Fred Depontee, the assistant director was Megan J. Stewart; the artistic consultant was Juel D. Lane, the production stage manager was Audrey A. Edwards. "YoungGiftedandFat" was performed Off-Broadway as part of the United Solo Theatre Festival in October of 2015 on Theatre Row, 42nd Street. It was directed by Sharrell D. Luckett, Guy Thorne, and Rahbi Hines; the musical director and lyricist was Rahbi Hines, the choreographer and media designer was Guy Thorne, the composer was Osbaldo Maravilla, the assistant director was Megan J. Stewart; the artistic consultant was Juel D. Lane, the production stage manager was Audrey A. Edwards.

2 The lobby display, "Fat Girl's Imagination," features various photos of Sharrell in oversized clothes eating, denying, or daydreaming about food.

CHAPTER 7

FAT GIRL FUTURITY

We've made it. We've made it to the end of this tale for now, and I'm still telling. Now that we've been where we've been, I want us to go where we're going, or where I think we're going. As I write, I remember my mother, who passed on her "writing spirit" to me, and reflect upon my instincts to write my life. I would witness her write herself into and out of situations, write herself notes to change past perceptions of her world; and now I imagine myself into the future, or I think I do. And often I ask myself who would my audience be, what would they think, what would they do with my thoughts? And would they know that these collected lived experiences are only fragments of who I am, captured instances, t(horny) coming of age stories, heartbreak, and hatred of self. Would they recognize the love in these pages too; love for my family, love for God, and love for self?

And what becomes of my perpetual youth, my recuperative giftedness, and my oscillating fatness of the mind and body? What do I make of an artistic transweight Black girl who has grown into a woman, and how would my young, gifted, and fat self function in the future? Further, what are my thoughts about the sharing of my lived experiences within the framework of critical autoethnography? How can the lived experiences of transweight folks and fat girls project new possibilities for the future? How can I get there before we get there? How do I envision myself? As these questions surfaced in relation to concluding this autoethnographic offering, a performative exchange emerged between my futuristic self and a young reporter. How could it not?[1] As my future self would have it, all of the telling, sharing, sacrificing, performing, creating, imagining, and so forth did not go in vain. It seems as if my lived experience echoed the experiences of others, and as the voice began to make itself clearer, my artistic impulses took over, and a transcription emerged; one that I have offered up to conclude this story ... for now.

★★★

You will write it down because if you don't write it down then we will come along and tell the future that we did not exist ... You will write it down ... so that in thuh future when they come along they'll know how they exist ... theyll know why they exist ...

Suzan-Lori Parks[2]

(*Sharrell's living room is cozy. She has rainbow colored ankle-length socks on her feet, and on top of that are some faux sheepskin cream leg warmers covering her calves. There are novels and academic books in neat clutters throughout her living room. On the coffee table sits three pairs of designer glasses. They look unworn. The sofa she is sitting on is blood red and has a heart shaped back. Her knees ache, and her face is just now starting to crease and wrinkle. Her hands rest in her lap and they look like the hands of a 30 year old. There is a journalist who sits adjacent to her in the firm dark gray sofa chair that is usually inhabited by Sharrell's poodle (Sherlock) who lays still on the floor, watching the journalist's every move. While anxiously readying the device to record the conversation, the journalist quietly admires Sharrell's skin and can't believe that she is in her mid-70s. The cover story on Sharrell's career and the 40th anniversary of the book release of "YoungGiftedandFat: An Autoethnography of Size, Sexuality, and Privilege" is almost complete. Record.*)

Journalist:	Thank you for sitting down again today with me Professor Luckett.
Sharrell:	Dr.
Journalist:	Excuse me?
Sharrell:	Dr.
Journalist:	Yes. Absolutely. Dr. Luckett.
Sharrell:	Folks ain't never wanted to call me Dr.
Journalist:	Apologies.
Sharrell:	You alright. (*She gives a small smile.*)
Journalist:	So, the 40th anniversary of *YoungGiftedandFat* is on the horizon. It's getting closer.

Sharrell: It's today ain't it?

Journalist: Well it's in a couple of months.

Sharrell: Naw, it's today. What is today?

Journalist: Dec. 31st.

Sharrell: Right. Dec. 31, 2016 *(pause)* is when I finished the book.

Journalist: Wow, I didn't know. I don't know if any of your readers knew.

Sharrell: That's why I'm telling you now. Write that down. *(The journalist scribbles on a pad.)* I'm telling you now. I don't just be talkin' for nothing.

Journalist: Right. Can you walk me through that day?

Sharrell: I had been working to finish the book, you know. The book was hard. Not cuz' it was a book, but because the stories, uhhh, the stories, it was hard to pick the stories to tell. And then it was hard to figure out how to tell the stories, and then sometimes I wouldn't like the stories, and then it was hard letting folks read the stories and me getting feedback on my life.

Journalist: Right

Sharrell: I mean, it's my damn life. Ain't no right way to tell it. *(She coughs.)* However I tell it, you should just take it.

Journalist: Take it how it's written.

Sharrell: That's right. And umm, but I guess I figured it out.

Journalist: You sure did. Your words have affected millions of readers.

Sharrell: *(Her face beams with sullen pride.)* Ummm hmmm.

Journalist: How does that make you feel? To have that type of impact?

Sharrell: *(Silent for a long time.)* I guess, I don't know. It's a lot to think about. A lot to take in. Honestly make me wonder why. Why? You know?

Journalist: Why?

Sharrell: Cuz' ain't nothing changed really. I mean, I was hoping after folks read the book that things would get better, be better. But all dese fat children runnin' round here, and I still hear folks calling them names. Mean thangs.

Journalist: Yes, but more fat positive organizations were formed. You partnered with Oprah. Your television show lasted many years. And your show on Broadway paved the way for a wave of successful musicals about size discrimation, and …

Sharrell: The songs were terrible. *(The journalist laughs.)* They were. God awful. What's that one? Ummmm … *(Lightly singing.)* "Here lies my belly, full of jelly … *(She finishes and they sing together.)*

Sharrell and Journalist: … blubbering along, fat makes me strong.

Sharrell: See, terrible! And they cast a bunch of white folks to be in the show.

Journalist: Well there were others who …

Sharrell: That's not the point. If you inspired by a Black person, and you make a show about some issues a Black person talked about, common sense should tell you to make it a Black show. But that's Broadway for you. See ain't nothing changed. And who directed the one with the 800 pound Black character?

Journalist: Kevin …

Sharrell: *(Cuts her off)*. Right, a white man. I can't figure out for the life of me why white folks feel like they can direct Black stuff. It ain't rocket science. Hire a Black person. Don't know nothing bout being Black, can't learn it, and that particular director wasn't fat neither. What a man know bout fat women issues?

Journalist: Well that one was the most successful.

Sharrell: It was. Yes it was, and so was "YoungGiftedandFat." The show I mean.

Journalist: Yes, let's talk about that. So you have finally retired from performing.

Sharrell: I ain't retired from performing. Always performing. Hell, I'm performing now. *(She smiles.)* That show has been put to bed though.

Journalist: Right, that's what I meant. The show. What was that like?

Sharrell: The whole experience? The tours? Writing it?

Journalist: I guess all of it. Well I guess, what was the most important thing you learned from doing the show?

Sharrell: Don't do it again. *(Laughs hard.)* I mean after the book came out, the show really took off, and I just tired myself out so. And every time I went some place, no matter the place, I would think, why did I think this was a good idea? *(Laughs.)*

Journalist: You didn't want to do the show?

Sharrell: It's not that *I* didn't want to do the show. It's that I wanted *somebody else* to do the show.

Journalist: Your show?

Sharrell: My show.

Journalist: But then it wouldn't be authentic would it?

Sharrell: Yes hell, I wrote it. I mean, find me a good, young actress. You know, young, and, ummm, interesting though. *(Reflecting.)* Nobody ever questioned the title after I got into my middle ages and a bit older, nobody questioned the "young" part.

Journalist: And why do you think that was?

Sharrell: I don't know. Maybe cause you can be young in spirit. Or maybe because that was just the name of the show, you know. Or maybe because "Young, Gifted, and Black" is such an endearing song. Everybody can sing it don't matter the age. But you know one time after performing my show in Australia, I believe, this young girl, lil fat chubby thang came up to me, so sweet, and she said, "Ms., Ms., why do you call yourself young?" And I didn't get mad. I really didn't have an answer for her. But I asked her, well what should I call myself? You don't think I'm young? And she just smiled at me. Might've been a little slow now that I think about it.

Journalist: So can we go deeper? *(Sharrell nods head slowly.)* Is there a story that you didn't want to tell, or grappled with a bit, or took out?

Sharrell: What kind of story you writing again?

Journalist: A cover story.

Sharrell: Ummm hmmm. Gone head.

Journalist: A story that you were apprehensive about sharing?

Sharrell: Well, all of them, you see. Anytime you start telling people stuff and airing yo laundry, you know, you can't control it when it's out there. Folks think they know you. They be looking at you weird. They think all types of shit about you. But umm, I … would … have … to … say … the virginity story. I mean, I remember one time Oprah told Alicia Keys to keep some things to herself. But you know I ain't never been afraid to talk about no sex. That don't scare me. So I let it stay, but I did keep some things to myself.

Journalist: So, how do you … *(Sharrell cuts her question off.)*

Sharrell: Now I did grapple with whether to include the passing of my mama in the book. I took it out at one point, then put it back

158

in, then took it out again. But decided to leave it in. I have to remind myself to let the mess land where it may. There is no way to clean up death. And losing her really affected me, and I really didn't start to deal with it until several years after the book came out. Cuz you know I took her out of my show too. Then put her back in ... *(Voice trails off. She pauses for a period of time.)* I just thank God that she saw me small, because my daddy didn't get to see the new me.

Journalist: Yeah, it's like we get to the end of the show and the book, and it becomes extra sad.

Sharrell: Yeah, it can be that way.

Journalist: Did it ever get easier?

Sharrell: Shoot naw. That's why I'm at peace with seeing sweet Jesus. I wanna see her again. I think she would be happy that I lived longer than she did, you know?

Journalist: *(Careful.)* And your daddy? Do you want to see him?

Sharrell: I do. But I painted a half picture of my daddy. He had many issues that I guess I don't like to talk about. Like, till this day my brother always points out that on Christmas our daddy wasn't never home; just messes up the whole day for me. But you know the book wasn't about him.

Journalist: Wow. Where would he be on Christmas?

Sharrell: Some things I keep to myself.

Journalist: Right.

Sharrell: Many things. Many, many, many things.

Journalist: But now Cheesecakes ...

Sharrell: Awe shoot, I knew you was going to bring her up. *(She smiles a wide smile.)*

Journalist: Of course, I have to. I can't come all the way here to wrap up our visits and not talk about Cheesecakes.

Sharrell: That name! *(Sharrell shakes her head.)* Lord, I truly was young and gifted. That ain't never a good combination.

Journalist: But I like Cheesecakes.

Sharrell: Oh, a lot of people liked Cheesecakes. That I know.

Journalist: So will we ever see her again?

Sharrell:	You wanna see this naked wrinkled body in a fish net onesie *(They laugh together.)* Nobody thought I was gonna do it, and I did it.
Journalist:	Strip?
Sharrell:	*(Quickly correcting the journalist.)* Dance. You know the strippers started calling themselves dancers. Seemed like a damn euphemism to me. But calling myself a dancer did make me feel better.
Journalist:	But it was an autoethnography.
Sharrell:	It was, but I still was doing the shit. I learned a lot too. Cheesecakes. Hmph.
Journalist:	*(Smirking.)* What did you learn Dr. Luckett?
Sharrell:	That I woulda been a stripper from jump if I hadda been skinny. *(They laugh.)* So I guess God saved me.
Journalist:	I guess he did.
Sharrell:	*She* did. But I think God love strippers too. God don't discriminate.
Journalist:	And Cheesecakes got her own book series now?
Sharrell:	That's right. You can't put all that in one book. And you know Cheesecakes was fully created after *YoungGiftedandFat*.
Journalist:	No I didn't know that.
Sharrell:	Yeah, she just appeared in one of my early videos, and then showed up again in the later ones.
Journalist:	Your webisode series?
Sharrell:	Yeah, ummm, *The Making of "YoungGiftedandFat."*[3]
Journalist:	Those are so funny.
Sharrell:	Ummmm hmmmm. I remember it, Uri McMillan had just released a book called *Embodied Avatars* and I was like that's what Cheesecakes is.
Journalist:	But she became real life?
Sharrell:	Yes, chile, after I lost all that weight and finally reached my goal, I had to show the world. *(She winks.)*
Journalist:	And you sure showed them.
Sharrell:	Ummm, hmmm, it was a study. You know, cuz' I was still trying to get tenure, but Cheesecakes was real.
Journalist:	Do you miss dancing? Cuz you were good!
Sharrell:	Hahaha! Surprised everybody! They was like, where did she learn how to do that? She gone lose her job! Ain't she a teacher? This seem too real? It *was* real, fools! Haha! *(Pause.)* I'm just not

sure autoethnography has a way to separate the real from the fake in folks. It's all real, and you're right there, remembering everything. But what's happening is really happening. And no matter what you write down, how you write it down or analyze it, you still did that *thing*, or you were with those people, and you can't fully explain your way into it or out of it. You just can't. But it became all too real for me. Too, too real. I didn't care bout being naked, but James, my husband, you know, he cared. That's what almost ruined our marriage.

Journalist: Really?

Sharrell: Yeah, especially when the kids started going to school. And I started dancing in the daytime on my days off.

Journalist: So you were ...

Sharrell: Doing stuff I wasn't sposed to be doing, but get outta my business. *(Laughs.)* That ain't in no book neither. And my agent said you was gonna be here all of ten minutes. I promise it's been an hour.

Journalist: Just a few more questions. Ummm, any more videos on the way?

Sharrell: Well, I was trying to make 50 so I could have 50 episodes. But my son won't help me. He keep saying he gonna help me edit it, but he don't. And then I don't think I like the footage. I look old to me, and fat.

Journalist: But you can be bigger now. You've earned it.

Sharrell: Naw, I look fat in all the footage.

Journalist: You still don't like looking fat?

Sharrell: *Being* fat. Looking, being, same thang.

Journalist: But you're not fat.

Sharrell: Yes, I am. Yes I am. Folks told me that lie my whole life. That's why I was fat for so long. They try to keep you fat. Don't want you to lose weight and look better than them.

Journalist: May I ask how did you keep the weight off for so long?

Sharrell: I used to say I don't know. You know, over the years folks have asked, and I say I don't know. But I'ma tell you a secret. There is no secret to losing weight. We all know how to do it. We just don't do it.

Journalist: And why do you think that is?

Sharrell: Well, everybody is not sposed to be small or slim, you know. I think it be the spirit. I think we know deep down inside that being fat is OK. That being fat is normal, but folks make you feel so bad about it, so you want to change.

Journalist: Like being Black?

Sharrell: No. Nothing like being Black. *(She is adamant.)* Write that down. Absolutely, nothing like being Black. Only folks who make that connection are the ones that don't want you to be Black, or the ones who want to get rid of Black folks, or those that don't wanna be Black. I ain't never, never thought about changing that, at all. My Blackness and my fatness are not the same. See that whole intersectionality stuff leveled the playing field. Like Black is like being like gender, is like being like poor.

Journalist: On the same level as fat?

Sharrell: Right, but that ain't so. Men and women ain't never fought. Fat and skinny folks ain't never fought. But them race wars, now them race wars was something serious. And who won? *(She laughs.)* Who won dammit? *(Laughs harder.)* I rest my case. Shit, talm bout race is constructed. I guess they got a constructed ass whooping then. Tuh huh, not in America dammit. Now everybody wanna be Black. That skin darkening cream is just crazy. *(Shaking her head.)*

Journalist: OK. OK. I see. Well, before I go I just wanted to read you some of what I have, based on the earlier interviews and make sure it's ok.

Sharrell: You sent me that email, and I read that email and added to it and such, and now you wanna read me the same thang?

Journalist: Yes ma'am. I mean, I worked on it some more.

Sharrell: Ok, I will hush, I'm listening.

Journalist: This is towards the end of the article:

There have been others that have tried to emulate her style, share her shine, but they have all gained their weight back, except Sharrell. I believe she has a secret potion somewhere hidden in her kitchen. She denies that. I believe she secretly had gastric bypass years ago. She denies that. I believe she doesn't eat. But she denies that too. And even in her senior years, at a size 8, she still identifies as a fat woman. Sharrell's autoethnographic study was the first of its kind. One that paved the way for hundreds of women (and men) to begin discussing the horrors of the aftermath of weight loss in the public sphere, ushering in the demise of Weight Watchers, Jenny Craig, Nutri-System, and even Slim-Fast. The field of Fat Psychology sky-rocketed and is still one of the most popular career choices today. And Luckett's study remains unique and at the forefront because she is one of the few to lose a considerable amount of weight, write about the good and bad consequences, and keep it off for decades. And as simple as that may sound, we all know keeping the weight off is a major feat. Folks just can't "shake the fat," as Luckett puts it. I wish I could tell you that Sharrell D. Luckett's journey has made her more accepting of her fat body, even now, but that's not true. I wish I could tell you that gaining weight doesn't bother her anymore, that she hopes to perform "YoungGiftedandFat" as a fat person, even in old age; that she loves her fat and slender self. But none of it would be true. The events surrounding her fatness and the neglect thereof in her youth and young adulthood traumatized her, and she is still not sure that she can ever fully release, forgive, and unhinge her soul. So she works through the muck.

Sharrell:	I do.
Journalist:	Finding sustenance in telling her story and massaging the wounds that herself and others may have from being young, gifted, and fat.
Sharrell:	and Black … from being young, gifted, fat, and Black.
Journalist:	She offers herself up.
Sharrell:	Myself up.
Journalist:	Her fat, her gifted, her Black …
Sharrell:	My magical …
Journalist:	Her magical story.
Sharrell:	Fatgirlmagic, that's what they called it back then.
Journalist:	Blackgirlmagic.
Sharrell:	…well then add Blackgirlgenius as well.
Journalist:	*(Laughs.)* She offers up her story for your survival.
Sharrell:	I am here.
Journalist:	She is here.
Sharrell:	I am still here. And I am enough. Write that down.

★★★

After that transcription spilled out of me, I wondered what book the reporter read, because it couldn't have included that script, could it? Cuz' that would be messing with the past. Or maybe she did read the future and simply fulfill the prophecy. The reporter doesn't mention the ending of the book, or how it ended, but it's clear that the book came out; but the narrative doesn't end. The narrative can't end as long as stories are shared. In my sharing with her, she is sharing with someone else and that way we carry bits and pieces of stories of each others' lives around.

I wrote unto myself a marriage, children, and what seemed like a very fun but fraught career of adult dancing. I wrote a world where Black people get their "get back," and where dark skinned becomes the desired hue. I wrote a world that has progressed in my eyes, yet this world was not able to reconcile the fat body. Even with the fall of weight loss empires, fat was still vilified. Maybe I could not imagine my way out of that pain. I could write my way out of heartbreak and racism, but I couldn't write my way out of fatness and losing my mother. So where does that leave me? Where does that leave us? What possibilities are there at the end of this textual, emotional and somatic journey?

I offer up space.

Space. *YoungGiftedandFat* makes space for other autoethnographers who are creatives; who float between fields; who are Black, who are fat, and inherently gifted. I call upon those who wish to go back and re(read) and respond or re(respond) to my invitation to reflect. I made space for you in my narrative. Put your words in this book or some other form of offering. That space was created for your voice. I can only hope that what you have read somehow positively informs what you share in that space, but then that is your space. Do responsibly with it what you will. Use it though, because then our worlds will be connected on the page.

Again. Space. There needs to be more stories from Black women about life. Period. More. Space. For. Us. Like fatness, our work needs to take up more space; space in scholarship, spaces on the stage, spaces at the leadership tables, mind space, worship space, outer space, inner space, cryptic space, genius space, magical space, and healing space.

That my conclusion concluded itself from a space of futurity, a future that is true for those characters, a future that will always be read as present tense, points to the power of capturing narratives on paper; and this overall offering points to the power of autoethnography. And even after all of this telling, I have much more to tell. But we are all complex in that manner. We all have too much to tell, many folks to tell on, and more than enough time to continue finding new ways to tell on ourselves. In this way, what you have witnessed is a snippet of a journey of someone who is YoungGiftedandFat; an enjambed descriptor that signals how I am and what I am as an intellectual, as an artist, and as a Black girl/woman. The methodology and methods of critical autoethnography allowed me to highlight the complexities and messiness of my construct of self. My Black, female, weighted self is wedged between these pages and my location in the world. My identity (YoungGiftedandFat) is enjambed not only in the ways that the written symbols are literally touching one another, but stuck together in a way that the computer processor underlines the enjambment letting me know that this intersectional word/identity is perhaps incorrect. The red, squiggly underlining suggests that I should look at these symbols a bit more closely, do a spell check or a grammar check because this word/identity is unrecognizable by the systems that have been put in place to dictate to me between right and wrong. The system would like for me to look for the correct word/identity; a word/identity already vetted by a system that would like to tell me what I am. But I resist, and continue to (re)make myself. This autoethnography joins other autoethnographic narratives that have the potential to enable more safe platforms for Black women and transweight identities to dialogue freely about the mythology of their bodies as it relates to size, sexuality, and privilege. And as this narrative comes to a close, it still feels like I have only scratched the surface of my being; the surface of being YoungGiftedandFat.

NOTES

1 This question is inspired by the work of playwright Tarell Alvin McCraney.

2 Suzan-Lori Parks, "Death of the Last Black Man in the Whole Entire World" In *The America Play and Other Works* (New York: Theatre Communications Group, 1995), 130–131.

3 Webisodes for *The Making of "YoungGiftedandFat"* can be accessed at www.sdluckett. com or at < https://www.youtube.com/channel/UC3bDCI2i4h9IGEFEoAIxttg >.

AFTER PIC

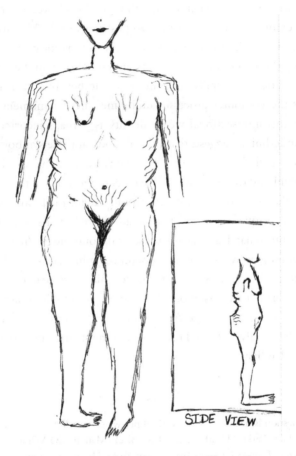

Figure Back 1: *After pic – author's illustration.*

INDEX

Note: numbers in bold indicate an illustration on that page.

abuse, verbal 1, 42, 82, 134, 146–148; by classmates 39–40, 82, 129; dealing with 76, 147; *see also* violence

acting 1, 4–5, 16; and training 4, 16–17, 120; *see also* performance

activism 12, 15, 16

advertisements 1, 9–10

African–American women *see* Black women

Afrocentricity 12, 16–17, 24

attention from men 34, 38; attitude to 83, 103, 108, 114; and fatness 1, 48, 82, 135–6, 138–139; after weight loss 75, 84–85, 103–104, 114

auditions 40, 43, 49, 137; and effects of weight loss 5, 69, 83, 140, 141; for *Fences* 80–3; for *Holding Up the Sky* 5, 68, 69, 140

autoethnographic performance 15, 16–17, 23, 119–122; inclusion of script 121–2, 123; script 127–51; "YoungGiftedandFat" 15, 23, 116, 119–120, **152**

autoethnography 3, 4, 9, 12–17; and activism 15, 16, 165; defined 13–14; and information gathering 19, 20–21, 22; and lived experience 13–15, 120–121, 154–155; and performance 8, 15, 21, 23; reasons for 15–16, 20, 154–155, 160–161, 164–165; and theater 16–17; and writing 154–155, 156, 158

autoethnography, evocative *see* storytelling, evocative

beauty 44, 69, 103, 110, 135–136; and advertising 9–10; and ambivalence about fatness 95, 100; belief in lack of 19, 69, 130; and casting as beautiful woman 5, 69, 140; desire to possess 40, 41, 52, 97, 128, 129; of mother 111, 114, 129–130; and need to be "nice" 84–85; sense of own 52, 77, 78, 129, 141; social constructions of 69, 121; validation by men 50, 75, 83, 106, 110–111

Black communities 9, 12–14; and slavery 3–4, 12, 43, 147

Black feminism 8, 9–10, 13–14; *see also* Black women

Black women 13, 16, 121; and lived experience 13–14, 24, 90, 154–155; and "passing" as thin 4, 7–8; and performance 8–9, 121; pride of 162, 163–4; and stories from 12–13, 14, 17, 164; and weight 3, 4–5, 9

Blackerby, Chris 21, 69, 77–79

blackgirl 14, 155

brother 31–2, 34, 35, 42, 132; relationship with 39, 52–53; and violence against 53, 55

Burch, Milbre 5, 21

Carver, Dr. Heather 5–6

clothing 99, 95, 103, 107; anxiety about fit 97, 106; anxiety about removing 72, 107, 109, 140; buying sexy underwear 99–100; and costume fitting for *Fences* 105, 106, 110; and costume for *Holding Up the Sky* 71–73, 140; disposing of

167

large clothes 100, 106–107; dressing for rehearsals 80, 106; and sense of feminine 2, 100; in stage show 127, 131, 135, 137–139, 147; after weight loss 18–19, 64, 66, 73, 84, 110; before weight loss 2, 40, 52, 138

Cogshell, Willie 21, 81–83, 86, 109; "coming out" to 111–112

Collins, Patricia Hill 3, 13

"coming out"; as depressed 50–51; as formerly fat 7–8, 21, 111–112, 144

data collection 15, 19–22

dating 2, 46, 48, 49–50, 128; when slim 143–144

depression 19, 50–51, 52; "coming out" with 50–51; and mother's death 115, 119; and relationship break-ups 66, 137–138; and self-loathing 51–52; and weight 3, 19, 115

diary see journal

dieting 3, 4, 18, 59, 62–66, 97, 128; determination to succeed 63, 64, 65; difficulties of 3, 9, 18, 62, 63, 65; dissatisfaction with dieting 147; excitement at weight loss 64–65, 144; and prayers to maintain diet 64, 65; and remembrance of father 64, 65, 148; and self-control 18, 63–64; and support 62–63, 65; and weight loss clinic 59–60, 116–117, 138–139; see also weight loss; weight maintenance

early life 30–35, 39, 54; and abuse around size 39–42, 82, 129, 146–148; and schooling 38–39, 40, 43; sexualization 30–32; and temper 33–34, 43

eating 56, 65, 79–80, 97; childhood meals 33, 43; for comfort 50; compulsive 19, 96–97, 145; Fat Sharrell and 90, 98, 101–103, 112; and hunger 62, 103; judgment-free 63, 108–109; junk food 33, 43, 108–109; monitoring 19, 79, 83, 101–103, 109; Skinny Sharrell and 95, 98, 101–103, 112; see also dieting

Excel Bariatric Center 59–60

exercise 64, 79, 91, 95, 96, 112; plans for 85, 97, 98, 117

experiences as Ph.D. student 68, 77; anxiety about weight gain 80, 140; auditions 5, 68, 69, 80–83, 140; determination to succeed 79–80; and fractured identity 95–9, 102–108, 112; further weight loss 79–80, 95; mother's illness and death 113–115

Fat is a Feminist Issue 1–2

fat jokes 82; encouraging laughter at fat self 39–40

fat rights 11–12

Fat Sharrell xx, 18, 89–91, 97–99, 101–103, 112; attitude to clothing being too tight 106–107; feelings about fatness 95, 96, 102; feelings about self 90, 95, 104, 105, 108; feelings about weight loss 95, 105; last photo of 60, 62, 67, 139; sense of having disappeared 95, 101; see also Liminal Sharrell; Skinny Sharrell

Fat Studies 10, 11–12, 15

father (James Luckett) 36–38, 118, 130, 142; absence of 159; ashamed of Sharrell 60, 139; death of 60–62; emotional unavailability of 55; influence of 55–56, 139, 146; relationship with 33–38, 52–53, 60, 139

fatness 19, 121, 127–128, 143, 147–148, 161; and awareness of male gaze 128; and childhood 23, 134; and denial of love 102, 110; effect on life course 1–2; effect on sexuality 19, 132–133; fat stigma 9, 10–11, 76, 148; as health crisis 1, 10, 12; male attitude to 134, 138, 148; meaning of 10–11; as moral crisis 1, 10

femininity 2, 9; and clothing 2, 100; performance of 5, 8, 69, 140

Fences (stage play) 8, 20, 21; anxiety about male gaze 107–108; anxiety about weight 105, 106, 109; auditioning for 80–83; and costume fitting for Fences 96, 105, 106, 110; and preparation for 85–86, 95, 97–98, ; and pride in own performance 110, 112; rehearsals 105, 109; and weight gain 96–97, 101–103, 107–108, 112

food see eating

Foucault, Michel 18

fractured identities 89–91; see also Fat Sharrell; Liminal Sharrell; Skinny Sharrell

God 47, 51, 142–143, 154, 160; as maker 102, 150; and mother's religion 134, 145–146; and praying for assistance 64, 65, 80; thanking for weight loss 64, 65, 80

Hagen, Uta 4, 5

health industry 11

Hendricks Method 4, 16–17, 120
Hendricks, Freddie 4, 17
high school experiences 134–135; desire
  for invisibility 136–137
Holding Up the Sky (stage play) 5, 20,
  21, 79; anxiety at not fitting role
  69, 140; auditions for 5, 68, 69,
  140; choreographing sex scene
  77–79; excitement at casting 70,
  140; expectations of ensemble
  role 68, 140; fear of exposing
  body 71–73, 140; performing
  femininity 69, 140; physicality of
  role 70–71
hunger 56, 89, 98, 149; as constant 128,
  149; "hungry" song from show 128;
  while dieting 19, 62, 102, 128; while
  maintaining weight loss 96, 101, 103;
  and starving self 3, 56, 95, 103, 107,
  112, 117

identities 3, 4; fractured 89–91, 121;
  multiple 89–90; weighted 4, 9, 165
identity 8, 12, 18, 165; and Hendricks
  Method 4; identity ambiguity 5;
  outsider-within 3; sense of 3, 5, 120
interviews 15, 21, 73, 79, 110–111; as data
  collection 20–2; interviewees 21; about
  physicality of character 70–71, 141;
  about size 69–70, 71, 81–82, 84, 141

Jamia *see* sister
Jones, Omi Osun Joni L. 17
journal 7, 8, 19, 22, 85, 119; diary as data
  20, 22; and fractured identities 91,
  95–99, 101–108, 112; video 20, 91

Kyree 30–31, 38–39, 130–33

Liminal Sharrell 95, 96, 105–108;
  and food 98, 102, 103, 112; as
  mediator 89, 90, 91; missing Fat
  Sharrell 107, 108; and attitude
  to size 97, 98–99, 102, 105;
  and suspicion of men's motives
  103–104; *see also* Fat Sharrell;
  Skinny Sharrell
lived experience 13, 23, 24, 154–155;
  and autoethnography 13–15, 120–121,
  154–155; and fractured identities 89–
  90, 154; of marginalized body 13, 23
loss of self 56, **67**, 89–90, 112, 139
Luckett, Beverly *see* mother
Luckett, James *see* father

maintaining weight loss *see*
  weight maintenance
messy texts 22, 23, 119, 158–159, 165; and
  self-reflexivity 24–25
Mia 73–77, 99
mother (Beverly Luckett) 21, 55, **118**,
  129, 148, 150, 154; ambivalent attitude
  of Sharrell towards 145–46; attending
  Sharrell's performances 109–110;
  beauty of 111, 114, 129–130; concern
  at treatment of Sharrell 129, 136; death
  115, 119, 158–159; illness 113–115,
  145; pride in Sharrell 110–111, 149;
  resemblance to Sharrell 129–130, 146,
  148; and Sharrell's sexual experiences
  30–31, 113, 131–132, 145; support of
  acting 43, 70, 79; support of dieting
  62–63, 145; support of study
  114–115, 149

obesity *see* fatness
Orbach, Susie 1
outsider-within identity 3

parents **118**; not physically resembling
  129–130, 146, 148; *see also*
  father; mother
"passing" as slim 4, 7–9, 139–140, 144
performance 3, 8, 40, 43–44, 49, 119;
  autoethnographic 16, 23, 119–123; and
  Black women performers 8–9, 121; of
  femininity 5, 8, 69, 140; in new body
  5–8, 21, 23; of slenderness 4, 5, 8, 102–
  103, 144; and theater training 4, 16–17,
  120; at university 69–73, 77–79, 80–84,
  109–111; *see also* "YoungGiftedandFat"
photographs 55; "before" 60, 62, **67**, 139;
  as data 20, 22, 109
poetry 16, 22; poems 22, 23, 43–44; *see
  also* script *under* "YoungGiftedandFat"
privilege *see* thin privilege

race 3–4, 162; *see also* Afrocentricity; Black
  communities; Black women
Rahbi 84–85
resistance 10, 13, 24; against society's
  pressures 121, 165
Robert 46, 49, 115, 137; acknowledgement
  of relationship 49–50; and end of
  relationship 65–66, 137–138
roles (acting); played by Sharrell 5, 69,
  81–84, 110–111, 140; preparation for 5,
  72; stereotypical for large actresses 4, 5,
  43–44, 68, 137

Ruffin, Clyde 21, 68, 71, 73, 111; and auditions 68–69, 81, 83; and covering of arms 72–3, 105; and ideal performer 70–71, 84, 141; and sex scene 77–79

Schechner, Richard 18
self, loss of 56, 89–90, 112, 139
self, sense of 5, 23, 50; as fractured 23, 89–91, 120
self-acceptance 95, 146, 150
self-confidence 41, 69, 115
self-esteem 83, 104, 108, 136
self-hate 1, 19, 50, 154
self-image 1, 34, 69, 140
self-love 19, 91, 107, 110, 137, 151
self-reflection 24–25, 50
sensuality 71, 121
sexuality 121, 141, 165; early sexual experiences 30–32, 130–33, 137; and body size 23, 132, 141; and brother 31–32; and loss of virginity 45–48, 158; and masturbation 31–32, 133; and mother 131–132, 145; and orgasm 32, 132–133; response to male desire 141–143; and sexual desire 39, 42–43, 44–45, 48, 52, 131; simulated sex 5, 77–79, 140
Sexuality Studies 15
sister (Jamia) 35–36, 62–63, 113–114
size prejudice 2, 10–12, 82, 121
Skinny Sharrell 87, 90, 95–99, 104, 108, 166; anxiety about weight 106–107, 112; critical of self 95, 96, 105, 112; desire to stay slim 95, 102; and eating 95, 98, 101–103, 112; and male gaze 91; see also Fat Sharrell; Liminal Sharrell
slavery 3–4, 12, 43, 147; and storytelling 12–13, 14
slimness 3–5, 60, 110, 141, 143–144; and "passing" as thin 4, 7–8, 139–140, 144; as performance 4, 102, 144; and thin privilege 3–4, 8, 82, 139
social drama theory 17
social justice 17; and rights 11–12, 14
storytelling 12–13, 14; evocative 14, 17
storytelling 12–13, 14; and Black tradition 13–14, 16
storytelling, evocative 13–14; and evocative narratives 14, 22, 115

Tandie 41–42
teaching 1, 7, 65

testimonial, script of "YoungGiftedandFat" as 121
theatrical training 4–5, 12, 16–17; Afrocentric 12, 16–17, 24; Hendricks Method 4, 16–17, 120
thick peculiarities 14–15
thin privilege 3–4, 8, 82, 139, 165
thinness see slimness
transweight 3, 9, 18–19, 22, 121; and Black women 9, 154, 165; identity as 20, 89–90, 120, 154, 165; as journey 17–18; and lived experience of 154; and performance 3–4, 120; and resistance 56, 165; and social drama theory 17
Turner, Victor 17
Tyra 50–52, 85

violence 40–41, 43, 134–135; fighting with siblings 36, 53, 55; see also abuse, verbal
virginity, loss of 45–48, 158
voice 13, 23, 164; and autoethnography 13–15; and identity 89, 90; and lived experience 14, 23, 155; and multivoiced texts 23–24

Waller, April 21, 73–76, 79
weighing; self 18–19, 65, 101; at weight loss clinic 59–60, 116, 139
weight gain 112, 115–117; anxiety about performance 140; and depression 115; and fear of costumes not fitting 105, 106–107; and preparation for Fences 85, 101, 112; and relationship break-ups 138, 145; and return to weight loss clinic 116, 117
weight loss 23, 85, 197–102, 115, 139–140; anxiety about gain 140, 144; dealing with body transformation 73–79; difficulty of 2, 10, 96–97; and hunger 3, 101, 102, 103; and identity 3, 4–5, 89; for opening of play 95, 102, 116; and performance of femininity 5, 8, 69, 140; and performance of slenderness 4, 5, 8, 102, 144; physical consequences 4, 5, 12, 81; positive consequences 139, 141; praying for assistance 64, 65, 80; psychological consequences 4, 60, 89–90, 97, 102, 149–150; and sense of loss 5, 23, 56, 67, 139, 149–150; social drama theory 17; and survival 59; and thin privilege

139, 144; trauma of 23; *see also*
Fat Sharrell
weight loss clinic 59–60, 116–117,
138–139; and photo 139; and
weigh in 59–60, 139; and weight
loss 139
weight loss industry 9, 11, 17, 18, 163
weight maintenance 23, 95–97,
140, 161; difficulty of 96–97,
145, 162–163; and dislike of

eating out 97; need for exercise
regime 97; need for monitoring
18–19, 97
Weight Watchers 17, 18, 163
Wilson, August 8, 81; see also *Fences*

"YoungGiftedandFat" (stage play) 15, 23,
116, 119–120, **152**; as ethnographic
performance 15, 16–17, 23, 119–122;
script 127–151